My Life In Yankee Stadium

*40 Years as a Vendor
And Other Tales of Growing Up
Somewhat Sane in the Bronx*

Stewart J. Zully

COPYRIGHT 2019 STEWART J. ZULLY

This work is licensed under a Creative Commons Attribution-Noncommercial-No Derivative Works 3.0 Unported License.
Attribution — You must attribute the work in the manner specified by the author or licensor (but not in any way that suggests that they endorse you or your use of the work).
Noncommercial — You may not use this work for commercial purposes.
No Derivative Works — You may not alter, transform, or build upon this work.
Inquiries about additional permissions should be directed to: info@StewartJZully.com

PRINT ISBN: 978-1-9834-2323-9

All photos courtesy of the author, except for the following:
  Ali/Norton program photo courtesy of George Kalinsky
  Identity Theft photo courtesy of Citigroup, Inc.
  1970 playoffs program photo courtesy of George Kalinsky
  James Gandolfini and the author photo courtesy of Ben Lipitz
  Author photo courtesy of Nick Toren

DISCLAIMER: Everything herein is my opinion regarding the people and events in my life. While every attempt has been made to verify the information in this book, neither the author nor the publisher assumes any responsibility for errors, omissions, or contrary interpretations of the subject matter. I have changed the names of some of the individuals that are part of my story. In no way should the reader infer that Major League Baseball or the New York Yankees have endorsed anything in or about this book.

CONTENTS

INTRODUCTION	V
WORKING PAPERS	1
A DAY IN THE LIFE	14
ONE SIZE FITS ALL	28
THE BALANCING ACT	42
THE SIXTIES	64
THE FANS	84
MY FELLOW VENDORS	99
SOME NIGHTS ARE DIFFERENT FROM OTHERS	114
NUMBERS	135
CHARACTER DRIVEN	146
POCKET MONEY	172
HOW TO BE A GOOD VENDOR	182
BRONX SCIENCE	196
THE FINAL SEASON: YOGI, IT'S OVER	205
NEW STADIUM, NEW ERA	217
AFTERWORD	234
ACKNOWLEDGMENTS	241
ABOUT THE AUTHOR	243

"The past is never dead. It's not even past."
—William Faulkner

INTRODUCTION

HAVING WORKED as a vendor in Yankee Stadium since 1970, I have come to realize that the steps and ramps have taken their toll and it's time to share my experiences with anyone who might be interested.

My life at the stadium gave me the best second job one could hope for. Through my teens, twenties, thirties, forties and, incredibly, into my fifties I was a witness to the most storied franchise in America, the New York Yankees.

Summers and baseball have been a major part of my life, helping me get through high school, college and my professional career. Growing up in the Bronx and vending at over 2500 events, I didn't want my stories to die with the old ballpark or frankly, with me.

Upon digging into my memory bank, I came up with an assortment of other tales from my past-my life growing up in the Bronx, my acting career, and other personal anecdotes which have made me who I am. I hope you enjoy them.

—Stewart J. Zully

WORKING PAPERS

WHILE GROWING UP in the Bronx in the sixties, I went to Yankee Stadium as often as possible. I would sit up in the grandstands for a dollar fifty a ticket, clutching a brown paper bag that often held a peanut butter and jelly sandwich and an apple, and enjoy the exploits of a good, and sometimes not so good, Yankee team.

I would always take along a notebook to keep score. There was no way I was going to pay fifteen cents for a scorecard for two reasons. 1: I couldn't afford it. And 2: I knew all the numbers and averages of the players by heart, since I had dreams of someday being the team's statistician.

One September day back in 1970, I was attending a game, and, while walking past an open doorway, I happened to peek in. I later discovered this room was known as a "station," the place where vendors came to pay for and replenish their product. To my surprise, who should be inside working but none other than my high school English teacher at the time, Mr. Keeghan. I was shocked to see him. I don't think I had *ever* seen a teacher outside of the school environment before—perhaps walking to his car after class in the parking lot once in a while, but that was it.

My immediate response was the obvious. "What are you doing here?"

Mr. Keeghan, a large man with an even larger heart,

fumbled a bit for the words, perhaps a little embarrassed at having one of his students catch him moonlighting. He quietly said, "Uh... I do this to make a few extra bucks in my spare time."

To be honest, I didn't know what he was talking about—he was a teacher, so I figured he already had a great-paying job. I just assumed he loved the Yankees and enjoyed coming to the ballpark, but all of a sudden my mind was racing with excitement. Maybe I could work there, too! Watch the games, meet all the players, and make some money. Why not?

1970 was the year *Let It Be* was released, The Beatles' last album before John and Yoko's marriage split up the band. I would often sit in my bedroom on a beanbag chair, listening to the record on a small, portable hi-fi. That year, my leisure time consisted of watching a new show called *The Odd Couple* on our black-and-white television set. I vaguely remember a news bulletin from Walter Cronkite or David Brinkley or some other man in a suit showing some horrible footage of an anti-war demonstration gone all wrong at Kent State University. There also was mention of the completion of a pair of tall buildings in lower Manhattan called the World Trade Center that would change the face of the city's skyline. I even spent time reading in the *TV Guide* about a show that was about to come on the air called *Monday Night Football* with somebody named Howard Cosell. I guess, at fifteen, I had a lot of time on my hands.

I grew up in a Bronx apartment in a lower-middle-class Jewish family, with two working parents and three older sisters: Janet, Robin, and Barbara. Sports were an important outlet for me, as I played Little League baseball and various street games whenever I could. I must admit I was pretty good, always hitting clean up in the batting order. In the street, we played stickball, with a broomstick and a pink Spaldeen rubber ball, and stoopball, with the same ball tossed against the edge of a building's steps or the front brick wall. In that game, the opponent needed to catch the Spaldeen on a fly or give up a single, double, triple, or home run with each successive bounce to the ground.

For most of my childhood, I shared a bedroom with my sister closest in age to me, Barbara, along with her dolls, her fan magazines, and her hairspray. When my oldest sister Janet got married and moved out of the apartment, Barbara gathered her stuff and shifted into Robin's room. Finally, I thought, I would have some space to myself. But my dad, who had an insurance business, moved his desk into my room and, since he came home around 3:30 every day, my afternoon privacy was gone.

About a year later, Robin was dating her future husband Alan, who lived in Brooklyn, so he often slept over in my room to avoid the long subway ride back home. So, at this crucial time in my life—my adolescence—it seemed as if I would never have any alone time... *ever*. I kept wanting to get out of there any way I could; I was tired of being dragged along to Brownie meetings and forced to tag along to numerous Sweet Sixteen parties. Sports, either playing it or watching it, was my best excuse to run out the door or into my private world of statistics.

I loved the minutiae of sports, as well. I would spend hours scouring newspaper box scores to follow my favorite players. Sometimes, I played dice baseball, which helped me escape the teenage angst of my three sisters. Dice baseball was popular in those days, as all that was needed to play was a pair of dice, a pencil, and paper to keep the box score.

There were many variations of the game, but my version consisted of rolling the dice and getting, for instance, a four. That meant a groundball. A five was a fly ball. A six was an automatic strikeout. Then I would toss the dice again and consult a page with a list of possibilities. For instance, for the fly ball, a two was a home run, a three was a double, a four was an out, etc. Then I would tally up the statistics of a full game, which could take me only about ten to fifteen minutes to complete. On family road trips, I would often pass the time by sitting in the back seat, playing dice baseball and keeping score in a small composition notebook.

When the game was over, I would add stats to a team sheet,

maintaining records of all the players including the pitchers. I would keep track of standings and league leaders in various categories as my hobby became a vital part of my childhood. My dad, however, broke my obsession down rather crudely by saying, "It kept him out of traffic."

The other board game I enjoyed at the time was Strat-O-Matic, which was a little more complex than traditional dice baseball because there were individual cards involved that used real statistics from the player's previous season. Dice baseball was convenient because it was so portable, but I loved Strat-O-Matic as well, because the scoring and stat keeping was much more sophisticated.

Opportunity can knock in strange ways, and on that one September day at Yankee Stadium in 1970, opportunity knocked so hard, in the form of my high school teacher, it would change my life forever.

With my little brown bag clutched firmly in my hand, I quickly asked Mr. Keeghan, "Uh, do you think you can get me a job here?"

Vendors were scurrying past him as he frantically jotted down names and numbers on some cards at his tall desk. Then he took a brief moment, leaned down, and whispered, "Talk to me tomorrow after class."

And so I did just that. But I discovered there was the little matter of getting working papers, which were issued to students who planned to work during vacations and after-school hours. In New York City, they could only be obtained at the age of sixteen.

Unfortunately, I was fifteen. But, being a kid in the Bronx with a solid connection like my English teacher, forging working papers was a snap. So, the next day, Mr. Keeghan enlisted the help of another teacher (whose name I forget, but I clearly recall him as being the mastermind behind the deception). This accomplice was straight from central casting—the short, intellectual, balding-with-glasses type. With their assistance, my birth date, writ large on some officious looking document, was doctored from my being born in 1955 and ever so carefully rewritten as 1954. Anyone who has ever attempted to alter ink with an eraser knows it is not an easy thing to do; I'm glad I had adult supervision guiding me along the way.

With this phony certificate firmly in hand, I signed up a week later and began my career as a vendor. Once I had gone through the orientation process ("Take the money-give the customer the item-move on"), I was handed my laminated ID badge, which had my picture on one side and my social security number and fake birth date on the other. In its own way, that badge, hanging around my little ol' neck, was my version of a "get out of jail free" card, enabling me to get out of my house and into the world of Yankee Stadium.

When I was hustling, running up and down the steps of the stadium, my badge often flipped around and exposed my birth date for the world to see. For many years I self-consciously had to spin it over, fearful that management would discover the lie about my age. Over the years I even imagined George Steinbrenner or one of his big, bad henchmen cornering me and asking to see my badge and "some other proof of age, *Sonny*."

Only when policy changed some years later, and when employee badges no longer had a vendor's date of birth printed on the back, did I allow myself to walk through the ballpark without a sense of guilt about my deception. So my career at Yankee Stadium began with ten years of espionage as I incessantly flipped that bogus badge around, shielding the truth because of some forged working papers.

I have always felt indebted to "Mr. K." and his bespectacled colleague from Dewitt Clinton High School for helping me rig my paperwork one late afternoon in the Bronx. After all, he helped me get a job that lasted over forty years.

As it turns out, my first day of work at the ballpark was not even at a *baseball* game but at a New York Giants *football* game. That winter of 1970, at age fifteen, I spent three Sundays selling either peanuts or hot chocolate and earned a grand total of $68. Working football games during those early years in the seventies was difficult for a number of reasons, but the main one was the weather: bitter, frigid cold. Maybe my skin was thin as a teenager, but I now have the utmost respect for people who work outdoors during the winter.

The ramps at the old stadium

For many games, it was also snowing or raining or just simply gray and depressing. And to make matters worse, the fans were mostly drunk men who were usually loud, boisterous, and unhappy that their Giants were losing, which they tended to do a lot. But tossing peanuts or handing over Styrofoam cups of hot chocolate, much of which spilled all over my uniform, was a lot of fun for a spunky kid like me. Navigating the raucous crowds certainly taught me how to develop my communication skills… fast.

I didn't make much money, but being with some of the most rabid, excitable, and knowledgeable fans on Earth was like attending a huge sports party. And it not only helped me elude my sisters and my suffocating home life, it also put a few bucks in my pocket at the same time.

The Giants are still known as the New York "football"

Giants, stemming from the fact that, until 1958, the New York "baseball" Giants played in the Polo Grounds in Manhattan. The word "football" was inserted to tell the difference between the two teams in conversation and the media. The "baseball" Giants, of course, have been in San Francisco for over fifty years, but the insertion of the word "football" still remains when mentioning the team that plays in New Jersey.

But I digress. Having worked three seasons of Giants games, with players like Fran Tarkenton, Tucker Frederickson, Homer Jones, and Pete Gogolak, I began my long vending journey and became linked, if only marginally, with the great history that is Yankee Stadium.

Football memories for me start with a man named Wilson, who used to give us our uniforms before each game. Jim Wilson was a great character—a burly, black, bald man in his mid-sixties who loved telling stories of his childhood in the segregated South and his "exploits with the ladies." I'm sure I am not the only vendor who got his first hint of the birds and the bees from Wilson. Until retiring in 1983, he slid my uniform pants and shirt across a counter to me with a warm smile and a chuckle, and my workday always began on a positive note thanks to Wilson.

Wilson seemed to be involved in a lot of things at the ballpark, some more kosher than others, and he was in many ways our unofficial mayor. He occasionally was running a smalltime card game or was selling day-old donuts for a dime. Rumor had it he used to work on his penmanship to copy the autographs of Yankee players, to make a buck or two to pay for his smokes. There were instances where he'd have boxes of new baseballs in the linen room and, during a game, would be replicating signatures to make, or create, "autographed" baseballs. (This was back in the day when autographed balls were *really* autographed by the players, not like today. Nowadays, machines do the replicating; back then, humans did. Wilson, I guess, was only human.)

Over the course of my years at the stadium, there was a wide assortment of items for sale in the locker room, such as baseball caps, Cuban cigars, bootleg videos, DVDs, the latest fashionable clothing, and much more. After one game, I came into the locker room and Wilson had managed to get ahold of an official football, known as "The Duke." He would often have something for sale in the locker room, perhaps some household item that had "fallen off a truck," as we used to say. But on this particular day, he had a slightly used practice ball that he'd procured from an equipment man in the Giants' locker room. This was the real deal: a genuine, official NFL football and Wilson was selling it for ten dollars.

I think every vendor that day had their hands on that ball—tossing it, running with it, dreaming about touchdowns with it, but ten dollars was about half a day's pay.

"C'mon, Stew," he said to me. "It's the chance of a lifetime."

But I passed. Of all the items on sale in the locker room through my many years as a vendor, "The Duke" is the only one I regret not buying.

Throughout its history, a number of events have taken place in the ballpark, including prizefights, college football games, and religious gatherings. My dad, who worked there in the thirties and once sold Babe Ruth six hot dogs before a game, told me many times of the intense rivalries between Army, Navy, and Notre Dame. He also told me that his brother, my Uncle Abie, worked there for a time. Even during my tenure, I helped get two of my nephews in when they were teenagers, but no one in my family hung in there nearly as long as I did.

Lenny, one of my dad's boyhood friends, also "woiked" in the stadium at one time, as he put it in his distinct "New Yawkese." He told me he was required to come in hours before the game to do prep work. All the vendors would have to sit in the stands and bag peanuts to sell later in the game.

"If ya didn't come early," he told me, "ya didn't woik dat day."

They also had to clean up the ballpark once the fans had left. Now, there are people who sweep up after a game throughout the night, but back then, the vendors had to do it.

In the early eighties, when my family had a party for my mother's sixtieth birthday, Lenny was there and told me about the old days, especially about the bottles (or, as he called them, the "bah-uhls"). I'm glad I had my miniature cassette tape deck with me to record this:

> I was dere from '34 to '41; and even Ebbets Field when dey started wit da lights in'39; soda was ten cents a bah-uhl, and lemme tell ya, I woiked my balls off. If you woiked a double header, and remember, dere was no radio or tv, so da joint was packed, dey wouldn't give ya back your street clothes unless ya cleaned da seats from da bah-uhls afta da game.
>
> Da garbage was da Yankees job but we vendors would carry a basket and fill it wit bah-uhls, den shove 'em in a big burlap sack—we'd just tro da bah-uhls in dere, and when it got full, some of us would lug it down ta da basement; we'd tro it into some hamper down dere—all broken glass and whatnot.
>
> Den, da next day, even if it was an off day and dere was no game, ya still had ta come in. You'd go down ta da basement, which was like a dungeon, like a real dungeon, and ya had ta separate da good bah-uhls from da broken ones—Coke here, Hires dere, Bruckner's over dere, and put 'em in cases, tryin' not ta cut your fingas as ya were doin' it.
>
> Now, I was a regular guy, woikin' every game, but if I didn't come in, I was <u>out</u>! Ya can ask my wife, I neva took a day off, **neva**. What's a headache? Who da hell knew from a headache? Now don't get me wrong, I was lucky. I woiked like a slave, believe me. Like a real slave, but I was makin' good money back den. Thirty-five bucks a week. Steady. I mean... where da hell're ya gonna make dat kinda money?

Years later, Lenny became a multi-millionaire by founding one of the world's largest leather clothing companies in the garment district. Another of my dad's stadium friends went on to become the president of Everlast, the boxing equipment company, so business know-how was certainly in the Bronx air at the time.

Since thirty-five bucks a week was "good money back den," cash was tight. My dad used to tell me, if the scorecard he was selling was three cents and someone in the middle of a row would buy one with a dime, Dad sometimes gave back only six cents change. That way, if an exciting play was occurring at that very moment, the fan might mindlessly put the change in his pocket and my dad would scurry off with the extra cent. But, if the fan began to count his change, Dad would quickly send the extra penny down the row. Life for a post-Depression-era kid, I suppose.

I would often think of him whenever I'd get passed a ten-dollar bill from a row of people for a nine-dollar beer. I'd s-l-o-w-l-y prepare to pass the single as I looked for a sign from the customer to keep it. I didn't hold back the money like he did, but times change. He waited on pennies, me... on dollar bills.

My dad told me he vended at many fights, which were common in the thirties, featuring Joe Louis, "The Brown Bomber." In 1976, I was fortunate to work the Muhammad Ali-Ken Norton championship, the only fight I ever vended. It was the third match between the two (each had won once), and it was a hard fought, though often sluggish, battle.

One of the perks of that type of event was I could go right where the celebrities were down at ringside, so long as I had an item to sell and kept moving—I even recall selling a hot dog to tennis great Jimmy Connors. Once the fighters had entered the ring, however, I was told to leave the field area. I then went up to the Loge section, which was the middle of the stadium, to stand and watch from a good vantage point. As far as I know, none of the vendors checked out early that night, since as long as we were still in uniform, we could take in the fight from anywhere in the ballpark.

Before the opening bell, Ali started to stroll around the ring and chanted, "Norton must fall!" as many in the crowd joined in the taunt. Yet for the first half of the fight, Ali hardly fought at all. He simply yapped at his opponent, hung on the ropes, shuffled a bit, and let Norton hit him, figuring that he would eventually tire him out. After jabbering away but not jabbing, some fans yelled to him, "Quit talking and fight!"

The cover of the program for the Ali/Norton fight

But Norton did *not* tire and, in fact, appeared to win most of the rounds. When the decision for Ali was announced, there seemed to be a shocked hush in the air, as if Norton had been robbed. I was a big fan of Ali's at the time, but many felt he got the unanimous decision because the boxing world favored him as defending champ over the less-exciting Norton.

That night, my respect for the sport was tarnished, and I still argue with anyone to this day that Norton beat Ali. Norton, I hear, argued it as well 'til the day he died. I later learned that neither of the two gave a post-fight interview in the ring, which is usually standard after a championship bout. The judge's decision apparently was the only thing that shut Ali up all night.

I worked other events, such as rock concerts featuring Pink Floyd, Billy Joel, and U2. Aside from T-shirts and hats, I recall selling condoms for the U2 concert. ("Hey, condoms here. Get your condoms!") The new stadium, aside from hosting hockey games, college football games, and other large-scale events, has brought Madonna, Paul McCartney, and hardcore heavy metal bands Anthrax and Metallica to the Bronx with, I am sure, many more acts to come.

In 1979, I had the honor to work when Pope John Paul II came to celebrate Mass. That day, I had souvenirs and sold all sorts of items like photos, pennants, and T-shirts. My stand was in the upper deck and I came out to the seats for a moment, so I could catch a glimpse of the Pope down on the field, while a security guard kept an eye on my inventory. I will never forget how quiet it was; more than 50,000 people perfectly still during the ceremony. I had been at the stadium for nearly ten years by that point and had worked World Series games and intense Boston Red Sox games, so I was used to hearing loud cheering and screaming, but I'd never been there when it was so eerily silent.

The next day, the Pope, after speaking at the United Nations, went to Queens and visited Shea Stadium. Fellow vendors who worked both ballparks often spoke of the fact that there were torrential rains all that day, which threatened to completely ruin the event. But, as those who attended his Mass at Shea have sworn to, when the Pope-mobile came on the field, the rain stopped and the sun subsequently came out as His Holiness hit the stage.

Being Jewish, I was nervous at the Pope's visit to the Bronx, wanting to say the right thing in the right way to the various nuns and priests at the event. As they passed by my stand in the hallway, I was on my very best behavior. One item I remember vending was a button for two dollars, which stated:

I GOT A PEEK AT THE POPE

I always tell my friends about how I broke the ice after the first solemn hour by yelling out, "Hey, rosary beads here. Rosary beads! No pushing. One at a time, Sister."

U2. The Pope. I guess business is business.

In 2008, the final year of the old stadium, Pope Benedict came to conduct Mass, but, unfortunately, I wasn't allowed to vend. In the twenty-first century, the Pope brings in his *own* souvenirs and his *own* vendors. I guess the papal business has become *big* business.

The city graciously welcomed him all around town, but I had to laugh when I was driving on the Harlem River Drive and saw a traffic sign posted that read:

> *Pope Visit at Yankee Stadium*
> *Use Mass Transportation*

Sounds like something Yogi Berra might've said.

Visits from the Pope, football games, and concerts aside, it was ultimately baseball that was the focus of my forty summers at the stadium. Every Memorial Day, Fourth of July, and Labor Day weekend for all those years, if the Yanks were home, I was there, vending to thousands and thousands of fans.

Over time, I have come to realize that Lou Gehrig, Joe DiMaggio, Mickey Mantle, and Derek Jeter all played their entire careers as Yankees, but not one of them worked as many games in the Bronx as I did.

A DAY IN THE LIFE

FRIENDS AND STRANGERS have often asked me what a typical vending day was like. This, or some variation of this, is what I told them.

At the old stadium, if a game started at 7 p.m., I was required to be at the ballpark at 5, giving the company time to assign me an item to sell and a station from where to get that item. The stations were spread out on different levels, so the employees could cover various sections without running into one another.

Once I got to the ballpark, I would show my badge and then fill out a card, writing down my name, company ID number, and social security number. On the back of the card, I would also jot down the product I would prefer to sell and the section I would like to work in, such as "Field 4-Beer" or "Upper 12-Hot Dogs." It was important to put a lot of choices down, since seniority (the company ID number signifies seniority; number one had the highest) dictated whose choices would get satisfied first. If my number had been eighty, for instance, all of the people with a lower number would get their choices granted before mine.

Almost all of the vendors with more seniority than me had scorecard gates at the entranceways to the ballpark, since time had taken a toll on their bodies and their days in the seats were over. Each time I came in to work during those last few years, I tended to get my first choice until eventually my shoulder, knees, and all the rest gave way and *my* days in the seats were over, too.

Many factors went into my choices. For instance, during the summer, the left side was the sunniest, so choosing that side of the field (the even-numbered stations) was best to sell cold items like soda, water, or ice cream. However, I can recall many excruciatingly hot 100-degree days when I opted for the odd-numbered right field side, just to maintain my stamina. Still hot, just not insufferable. Also, in scorching weather, I saw a lot of ice cream melt in my bin, making it a tough sell. And, depending on who was my checker in the station that day, returning the melted product could often be a major hassle.

Prior to getting into the union in the mid-seventies, it wasn't quite so simple to get a day's work. The foreman, a rather dumpy, thinly haired man named Lew, would ask all the vendors to stand across the street from the employee entrance and, at his whim, would call people over by name. Then, he would hand them a card to fill out; at that point, they knew they would be working on that particular day. Since fan attendance was not very strong and the vendor's union hadn't even existed at that time, there was no such thing as guaranteed work.

Those who sucked up to Lew quickly became his favorites. I was not one of them, but one day, he was looking at me and indicated with his finger that I should step over to him. I hadn't worked in a number of days so I thought, *Great, I'm getting in.*

When I got across the street he said, "What's your name again?"

I told him, he nodded in acknowledgement and then pointed at me to go back across the street, which I sheepishly did. I didn't work that day. *Ugh.* While enduring those frustrating early years at the stadium, trying to salvage a day's work, I never would have thought I'd last as long as I ultimately did.

After filling out my card and handing it in to whoever was in charge that year, I went downstairs to the linen room to get a uniform, a pair of white pants, and a standardized company shirt. Wilson was there when I started, but, over time, there were at least a dozen different employees running the linen room and handing me my clothes. Every vendor was required to wear this uniform, along with a company hat, which was assigned at the beginning of the season. When I first started, the hat had "Canteen" emblazoned on it. Then, after a corporate merger, it was "Volume Services," and later the company changed its name to "Centerplate." In the new stadium, with a different corporation in charge, it is the plain, navy-blue, standardized Yankee hat with the famed, interlocking N-Y. An apron to hold change, which was also given out at the beginning of the season, was optional.

Often, the linen room ran out of sizes, because the company, whatever they were called, saved money by not laundering the pants on a daily basis. Latecomers often got stuck with pants three, four, or more sizes too large. I hated when it happened to me, but I admit, it was funny seeing other vendors in those hip-hop-style pants, especially when they forgot a belt and were forced to use string or rope to keep a fifty-four-inch pair of pants from sliding down to their ankles. If I couldn't find enough string to fit around my waist, the trick was to simply run whatever I had through the two loopholes right above the zipper. Six inches of string or rope was enough to pull tight enough to tie and prevent an accident.

Once into uniform, the next hour was free time to hang out. This was when the powers that be were sorting through the cards, to figure out who would be working where and selling what.

The stations were Field 4, Field 11, Main 19, Main 20, Loge left, Upper 1, Upper 12, Upper 19, Upper 28, and the bleachers. The numbers signify the sections where these stations are located, with the uppers having four stations, since it had the most seats.

During the hour wait is when vendors had the opportunity to have a bite to eat, schmooze with friends, play cards, read, write, do homework, flirt, etc. Sometimes, we would hang out in the locker room or the bleachers and watch batting practice.

Each year would bring some new female vendors who might attract a bit of attention, at least until May or June, when everyone sorted out who's who and what's what.

The Yanks warm up before the gates open

Occasionally, during this break, I would go to the upper deck and jog through the empty stands before the gates opened and the fans came in. I would hear the chatter during batting practice while running within the sections from one foul pole to the other. Jim "Catfish" Hunter, aggressive competitor that he was, threw a ball up there one time, trying to hit me just for kicks. Fortunately, he missed. I remember yelling down at him, questioning what the hell he was thinking, and he seemed to guiltily sulk off into the outfield, realizing he was wrong. Nevertheless, I scooted out of the seats before anyone from management found out that I, a low-on-the-totem-pole vendor, had yelled at a Yankee.

For many, vending is a second job, so this downtime was a good opportunity to catch up on business, make phone calls, or do some paperwork. Over the years, I have known vendors who have been students (high school, college, grad school), teachers, principals, accountants, med students, architects, financial analysts, cops, actors, and even a comedian or two. I later learned that Tom Hanks was a vendor in Oakland before he became the Tom Hanks we know now. One of my fellow vendors installed video games in laundromats, and another was an electrician who fixed audio equipment on the side. Unfortunately, he tended to get a little backed up, so I could give him a broken radio in April and might not get it back until after the All-Star break in July.

The vending corps is a cross section of gritty, hard-working civilian life. One vendor, who lived a little more than an hour north of the stadium, worked as a corrections officer in a state prison. He woke up at 5, got to the prison at 6:15, was there until 2:30, drove down and got a quick bite to eat, worked a night game until 9:30, and then checked out and drove the sixty miles back home. When the Yanks had afternoon games, he took a vacation day, which is a very common stratagem amongst vendors who have second jobs. My prison guard colleague was one hard-working individual, and I doubt he would have been able to put his kids through college or buy a house if it weren't for his vending job to augment his pay.

Years ago, there was a vendor who had a high position with the IRS, and he often told me about his off-season adventures hunting tax felons around the globe. One winter, he spent three full months in Thailand, covertly tracking down a scofflaw. When I saw him the following opening day and asked him about his pursuit during the off-season, he told me he'd "got his man."

Once the call sheet had been completed, a list was posted of where the vendors were to be stationed for the game. This was known as "call time." Someone would stand in front of the day's vending corps, some days numbering as many as 125-150 vendors, and yell out the stations, the products, and the names, such as:

FIELD 4:
   BEER – Wilson, Davis, M. O'Toole, J. O'Toole
   HOT DOGS – Klein, Winston, Rayfield
   PEANUTS – McKoy, Edmonds, Gomez
   SODA – Reese, Steinblatt
   ICE CREAM – Gottlieb, Fitz

Once I knew where and what I'd be selling, the next trip was to the money room to get a price badge. If, during a prior game, I had sold soda and today I was selling ice cream, I'd simply exchange one badge for another. If my item today was priced at $3.50, I would get a few rolls of quarters, perhaps fifty singles, and some fives and tens, in order to make change. When I first started, a can of beer sold for sixty-five cents, so I needed to get rolls of nickels and dimes, as well. One season, ice cream sold for the ridiculous price of thirty-two cents. Needless to say, making change that summer was a big, fat pain in the ass.

The standard items to vend are peanuts, hot dogs, beer, soda, and Cracker Jacks. Other products I have hawked (vendors have often been referred to as "hawkers") include pizza, pretzels, knishes, egg rolls, ice cream (sandwiches, cones, cups, bars, and sundaes), freeze pops, frozen lemonade, cotton candy, Sun-Dew orange drink (that didn't sell), licorice (even worse), and M&M's (in the heat of summer—fuggettaboutit). Without seniority, you might get one of these lesser items and become frustrated as fans yelled, "Hey, Good & Plenty guy! Get outta the way!!"

Every so often, we would be selling different brands of beer, dependent upon which distributor gave our parent company the best deal during the off-season. Through the years, I sold Bud, Bud Light, Heineken, Corona, various Millers including Miller Genuine Draft, Beck's, New Amsterdam, Red Dog, Foster's, and even the alcoholic product called Mike's Hard Lemonade.

Let's assume I had been assigned peanuts today in Main 20. After getting my price badge and some change, I'd go up to the station, which was on the main level between the visiting dugout and the left-field foul pole. Approximately fifteen minutes before the start of the game, I started to vend.

Different products sold better at different times. While the new ballpark has a whole range of items for the fans to eat, the limited choices at the old stadium brought some predictable selling patterns for the vendors. Peanuts usually were pretty consistent sellers throughout the game, as was beer, whereas hot dogs tended to get busy only during the first few innings. The reason for that was many people got to the ballpark with the idea of having a few dogs as their dinner. But by the second or third inning, hot dogs became a dead item.

Ice cream, which didn't sell too briskly at the start of the game, became popular around the third or fourth inning, since the fans had had their meal and were looking to satisfy their sweet tooth or get a "second wind" from the sugar rush. The new stadium offers ice cream stands throughout the ballpark, but back then, the ice cream vendors would often put off going out until the top of the second inning, because they knew the variables for when their item would sell best. Obviously, when it is very hot, new stadium or old, ice cream, soda, and water sell consistently throughout the whole game.

Once getting up to Main 20, I would see who was the porter handling the nuts that night. When I needed a box, he'd get it from the back of the commissary for me. Before walking out the door, I would see someone standing behind a tall desk. This is the checker (Mr. Keeghan was my checker once in a while), who marked down on a card that I had taken a box of peanuts. It was, and still is, this person's responsibility that every one of the peanut boxes in the commissary, sometimes as many as fifty or more, was accounted for at the end of the night.

Peanuts are a tradition at the ballpark; a fun item to sell, as they can be tossed, and the fans take great delight in catching the bag. Once I had sold my box, I would head back to the station, break down the carton by folding and flattening it so it could be discarded easily, and then I would walk over to the other side of the tall desk, where a banker was there to take my money. If a bag of peanuts was $4 and there are 36 bags in a box, I handed $144 to the banker. He would then initial my card as "paid," and I would be free to get another box and repeat the process.

Since it got extremely hectic in the station, I always waited for confirmation that the figure I'd handed over was correct and that I'd been properly credited. A lot of money gets counted during the course of a game, and honest mistakes happen. That's why I was to state my name and how many units I had sold when I walked out the door. Calling out "Zully, 2-1," which gave my name, what box I was about to go out on, and how many I had paid for (out on my second, paid for one), became standard procedure.

A card to be filled out by the checker

Often, when it got busy, the banker might let me pay after every two boxes, so I might be saying "Zully, 4-2," so it was a good idea to keep everyone honest by making that announcement and not have a problem at the end of the night, when I was checking out. Occasionally during a homestand—the series of home games usually played within six to twelve days—discrepancies occurred regarding whether someone paid for the correct amount of trays. These standoffs between checkers, bankers, and vendors got, let us say, quite testy, since a day's pay could be on the line.

Basically, a vendor is a middleman. I take a box of peanuts, I go out and sell them, and then I bring the money back. Simple. By the end of the night, which in the case of vending peanuts is the top of the eighth, I might have sold five boxes. This meant I had turned in $144 five times for a total of $720. Depending on my seniority, which defined what my percentage rate was, my commission was tallied and put on my card. At this point, the checker signed it and handed it back for me to also sign. I was then given a slip, my receipt, and I was free to go down to the locker room and change back into my street clothes to head on home.

But wait! Not so fast. There was still one more thing to do, which was to deal with the porter.

If my item for the night was hot dogs, the porter in the station had a lot of work to do to help me prepare. He needed to heat up the frankfurters in a large vat of boiling water, and fill my bin with mustard packets, napkins, rolls, and a long, wood-handled, stainless steel fork. If I sold beer, the beer porter might need to mix different types of beers in the bin (regular Miller with Miller Light, etc.), or help me by bringing ice up to the station so the product stayed cold.

Years ago, some stations didn't have proper refrigeration to store cases of beer, so we sold "drips"—twelve- and, later, sixteen-ounce cups of beer that were filtered through a dispenser connected to large kegs. The porters would get to the station early and cup up the aluminum trays, which were then passed under the dispenser that would fill a row of four cups at a time. Then, the porter would place the full tray under another machine that would vacuum-seal a plastic film on top of the cups, stack the trays, and do it again. The porters dealt with a lot of frustration back there, as sometimes one line from the dispenser would get clogged and emit pure foam through the antiquated machinery. Then he had to refill cups from the good lines and switch and replace the bad ones.

It was a slow process, and, when business was brisk, I would often find myself on line, waiting for my next beer tray. Everyone grumbled, as fans would start lining up outside the station. Tempers flared, as we knew valuable selling time was ticking and commissions were being lost.

We tended to work with the same vending crew each night, since we were all close to each other in seniority, and some guys were known to jump the beer line. We nudged, we pushed, and we stood our ground, not wanting to lose our place to an overeager vendor. And our pride was always on the line, as we all wanted to be the "top man" working out of his or her station. Whenever I headed home, knowing I had sold more cases than anyone else that game, I must admit I slept better that night.

The porters' work was very methodical but hazardous, as the sealer machine would often burn their fingers. In addition, the beer would spill all over us vendors. One co-worker told me he was pulled over while driving at the Whitestone Bridge after a game and accused of being drunk, because his car smelled of alcohol. It took him ten minutes of pleading with the officer, explaining to him exactly what he did for a living, to prevent being arrested. I hated the hassle of drips, and all of us were relieved when cans and plastic bottles made drip beer a thing of the past.

For doing so much work for us vendors, the tradition at the end of the workday was to give a tip to the porter. This tip is known as "subway." Even a tip from the fans out in the seats is also known as "subway," and it has been called that for as long as anyone can remember. I assumed it got that name because it was a little way of helping workers get on the subway at the end of the night. While vendors were very happy to get it, porters *relied* upon it to boost their modest, fixed, day's pay.

The standard "subway" the porters had grown to expect went up as a vendor sold more and more product, so peanut and soda vendors therefore gave less than the hot dog and beer vendors. Some porters used to stand by the door to influence donations. Many times, after "hitting the cup" upon checking out, I would often lightheartedly hear, "Hey, where's the rest?" One such porter grew to be so good at squeezing out more and more "subway," his nickname was "Reverend Ike," an evangelist of the day, who claimed, "The root of all evil was the *lack* of money." I can still hear that porter now: "How 'bout a little donation for Reverend Ike?"

One tricky aspect of subway was that my fellow vendors would get mad if I contributed *too much*. In other words, the bar couldn't be set too high, because then the porters would have a standard they would want all of us to meet. Usually, we vendors would get together and come up with a common figure to give for each tray, box, or bin sold, to avoid this predicament.

Back when we used to sell cans, some vendors would occasionally not pour out a full beer into a customer's cup. The haste of quickly serving gave way to leaving a little bit in some of the twenty-four cans in their case. If, during a pour, there was a lot of "head" and the customer was in a hurry, there tended to be a little bit of beer left in the can. Then there'd be a few drops to top off into another customer's cup, to help gain a little bit more of a "subway" from them. This extra service in turn helped vendors deal with "Reverend Ike" later that day. Many of our regular fans were wise to this tactic and would make sure the whole can was poured, sipping off the foam in their cup so they would get all the beer they had paid for.

Hot dogs were actually accounted for by buns, not by dogs. One or two franks might be missing from the net of thirty-six, yet the buns were packed in cellophane by the dozen, which was a more precise count for the checker. If a customer didn't want a bun or wanted two dogs in *one* bun, a vendor could make a few bucks by saying at the station that the bin was short by a dog or two. By simply showing a bun to the checker, the vendor would get a credit. Unfortunately, these little tricks of the trade, essentially petty theft, would get these vendors suspended or fired, so the practice tended to be short-lived.

In 1988, I was approached to write and produce a training film for incoming vendors, showing how a typical "day in the life" would go. This industrial film was to be a primer shown to new employees at orientation meetings. Many vendors bumbled their way through their first few games and often didn't find their way back to the stadium after only one or two homestands, so the parent company thought this would be a good idea for these new workers.

After I shot *Service with a Smile,* I needed to find someone to do the film's narration. This was not going to be easy, since my small budget only had $150 left for someone to do the job, which was going to be two full days of work.

Around that particular time, I happened to be riding the number 2 train on the west side of Manhattan, wondering where I was going to find my narrator, when I happened to bump into a friend who I'd gone to school with years earlier. Standing in the subway car, catching up with him about old times, I suddenly came up with an idea. He had a terrific speaking voice, so I gave him a page of dialogue I had written for the film and said, "Wilbur, read this for me, will you?"

As some of the passengers gave us some odd looks, he whispered in my ear, "We are dedicated to our customers and we want them satisfied every time they come out to the ballpark. So remember, always serve with a smile."

It was kind of funny, now that I think about it, having him read for me between 72nd and 42nd Streets on an express train at rush hour. It was a case of auditioning not Off-Broadway, but *under* Broadway. And by the time the train pulled into Times Square, he had the job.

Once a homestand was over, I would expect a check in about seven to ten days. A baseball schedule is usually one week of home games and one week of away games. Often there were no days off, so, with high seniority and working every game, I might go as many as twelve or thirteen straight days. During hot stretches in July or August, these tended to be a little arduous as the steps seemed to get steeper as the week wore on. In addition, working a day game following a night game could be exhausting. Thankfully, once the Yanks went on the road, I would be off as long as two weeks and was able to catch up on my sleep and get my laundry done.

I always kept a Yankee schedule in my wallet or date book, so I knew what I was doing from April through September. When many of my friends were going to a barbeque for July Fourth or the Memorial Day weekend, I might have had a day game versus the White Sox. My birthday is in August, but holidays and birthdays grew to be somewhat meaningless for a dedicated vendor.

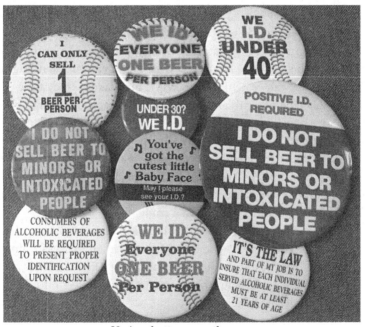

Various buttons over the years

two. By simply showing a bun to the checker, the vendor would get a credit. Unfortunately, these little tricks of the trade, essentially petty theft, would get these vendors suspended or fired, so the practice tended to be short-lived.

In 1988, I was approached to write and produce a training film for incoming vendors, showing how a typical "day in the life" would go. This industrial film was to be a primer shown to new employees at orientation meetings. Many vendors bumbled their way through their first few games and often didn't find their way back to the stadium after only one or two homestands, so the parent company thought this would be a good idea for these new workers.

After I shot *Service with a Smile,* I needed to find someone to do the film's narration. This was not going to be easy, since my small budget only had $150 left for someone to do the job, which was going to be two full days of work.

Around that particular time, I happened to be riding the number 2 train on the west side of Manhattan, wondering where I was going to find my narrator, when I happened to bump into a friend who I'd gone to school with years earlier. Standing in the subway car, catching up with him about old times, I suddenly came up with an idea. He had a terrific speaking voice, so I gave him a page of dialogue I had written for the film and said, "Wilbur, read this for me, will you?"

As some of the passengers gave us some odd looks, he whispered in my ear, "We are dedicated to our customers and we want them satisfied every time they come out to the ballpark. So remember, always serve with a smile."

It was kind of funny, now that I think about it, having him read for me between 72nd and 42nd Streets on an express train at rush hour. It was a case of auditioning not Off-Broadway, but *under* Broadway. And by the time the train pulled into Times Square, he had the job.

Once a homestand was over, I would expect a check in about seven to ten days. A baseball schedule is usually one week of home games and one week of away games. Often there were no days off, so, with high seniority and working every game, I might go as many as twelve or thirteen straight days. During hot stretches in July or August, these tended to be a little arduous as the steps seemed to get steeper as the week wore on. In addition, working a day game following a night game could be exhausting. Thankfully, once the Yanks went on the road, I would be off as long as two weeks and was able to catch up on my sleep and get my laundry done.

I always kept a Yankee schedule in my wallet or date book, so I knew what I was doing from April through September. When many of my friends were going to a barbeque for July Fourth or the Memorial Day weekend, I might have had a day game versus the White Sox. My birthday is in August, but holidays and birthdays grew to be somewhat meaningless for a dedicated vendor.

Various buttons over the years

Many of us prided ourselves on not missing any of the eighty-one regular season games during the course of the season. One year, I had a souvenir stand, and I told a fellow vendor my sister was getting married on the same day as Bat Day, which was an extremely profitable game for us souvenir men at the time. His response: "I hope she understands."

If the Yanks made the playoffs, there were more games into the month of October, as long as the team kept winning. During the playoffs and especially during the World Series, the games were exciting and the money was obviously better than during the regular season, as the "high rollers" started to show up.

One World Series I unfortunately had to miss was in 1977, when the Yanks played the Dodgers. I contracted mononucleosis after the playoffs and had to skip the final two games in New York. I'd been waiting all season for the playoffs and World Series, and the timing of my illness could not have been worse. I had a profitable souvenir stand at the time, and I told my doctor I could make my month's rent in just one game, but he advised me not to do it, so I listened to him.

Mono really knocked me out, but it was tough to stay in bed and watch the World Series in my pajamas. In fact, after working at Yankee Stadium for so long, whenever I am sick and catch a game on television, it can be a very strange feeling. And the odd thing is I usually find myself not watching the game but watching the vendors.

"Oh, look at that. Barney got beer behind first today."

How does that one go? "You can take the boy out of the Bronx, but...."

ONE SIZE FITS ALL

ONE DAY IN THE late seventies, when I was shut out of selling food, someone told me to "go over to the souvenir room—they may need some vendors." That was when I first became aware of souvenirs and the art of carrying and selling large foam fingers through the stands. Over time, I moved up the souvenir list and had my own booth for a number of seasons.

When I had my souvenir stand, I was required to be one of the first to arrive at the ballpark and one of the last to leave. I had to check in about two hours before the gates opened, to replenish stock from the souvenir room and get to my stand to set up for the game. Once the game started, the souvenir room would occasionally make "drops" to my stand with certain items, but I always had to come in early to load my inventory properly.

In the old stadium, when the game was over and the place was completely cleared of fans, I needed to "break down" my stand, bring my merchandise to the basement, and turn in the day's take to the money room. In those days, I didn't need to give a precise figure after each game when handing in money. However, once the homestand ended, I was required to do a full inventory and then balance out the books. That day, usually a Sunday, could be extremely long, as every T-shirt, every hat, every keychain, every single item had to be counted. Even now, when I walk into a store that has a lot of stock—anywhere, any store—I think of those long, late Sunday afternoons in the Bronx.

The Yankees are, as their marketing department has reminded us for many years, "the most storied franchise in sports history." Because of their great legacy of championships and Hall of Fame players, fans who come to the Bronx like to take home a souvenir of their visit. In the nineties, when I had my stand, I thought I had an exhaustive amount of merchandise, but that was just a fraction of what is being marketed today. Currently, the Yankee Clubhouse stores in New York City or the main gift shop at the new stadium sell a vast amount of items, from golf club covers to gardening tool bags, all with the famous interlocking N-Y somewhere on them.

Nevertheless, I thought I had a vast array of items, so here is just a partial list of what I carried:

* Autographed baseballs (printed *facsimile* autographs, of course)
* Official League baseballs (the kind used in a Major League game)
* Logo baseballs (a cheap alternative to the official ball)
* Plastic baseball holders (different styles)
* Commemorative baseballs (a rubber-stamped photo of something memorable e.g., a perfect game, a retired player's big day, etc.)
* Player keychains (with the picture of a current player in a small, acrylic casing)
* Keychains with small bats attached to them
* Yankee bottle cap openers
* Baseball card sets of roughly twenty cards (in a plastic case)
* Ceramic coffee mugs (difficult to store and keep from breaking)
* Wristbands (interlocking N-Y stitching)
* Batting gloves (one glove to a package, left or right)
* Baby bibs (various styles)

* Bobblehead dolls (generic Yankee ceramic dolls dressed in either white home uniform or road gray; also difficult to store and keep from breaking)
* Blankets
* Woolen ski caps (one size fits all)
* Official Yankee caps (sized)
* Yankee standard caps (one size fits all—when a customer was in a rush and asked for a hat, this is what I gave them)
* Infant caps (one size fits all infants)
* Caps with specific player numbers on them
* Caps with specific player *pictures* on them
* Striped caps (one size fits all)
* Stonewashed caps (one size fits all)
* Bucket caps (fisherman caps in various colors-one size fits all)
* Yankee Stadium "Built in 1923" caps (one size fits all)
* Mesh caps (one size fits all)
* Caps with sewn-on commemorative patches (World Series, All-Star game, etc.)
* Low profile caps (with an interlocking N-Y somewhat smaller than the standard interlocking N-Y)
* Caps with interlocking blue letters on a white background
* Caps with interlocking white letters on a blue background
* Stuffed Yankee dolls
* Stuffed Yankee bears (small and large, brown or white)
* Stuffed Yankee monkeys (various colors)
* Scorecards
* Yearbooks
* Media Guides
* Suntan lotion (not sun*screen*; sun *lotion*)
* Hair scrunchies (red and blue, red and white, blue and white, blue and red)
* Sunglasses (with the Yankee logo on it)

- Replica Yankee batting helmets (plastic)
- Small Yankee batting helmet banks
- Magnets (various, for the refrigerator)
- Individual player plaques (essentially a baseball card with a solid-wood backing, suitable for hanging)
- Individual 8-by-10-inch player photos, including old timers like Mickey Mantle and Babe Ruth (also suitable for framing, then hanging)
- Team photos (frame away, fans)
- Large-sized posters (I hated those, because they were difficult to keep from getting torn)
- Pink children's T-shirts with the word *Yankees* written across the chest (in various sizes)
- "Property of the Yankees" T-shirts (infant, children and adults, sized up to double-X, long or short sleeves)
- Navy Blue batting T-shirts (infant, children, and adults, with the interlocking N-Y on the front, no name on the back; long or short sleeves)
- Player name shirts (same style as the batting T, but with a player's name and number on the back, children and adults, sized up to double-X, in blue and pink—*ugh*!)
- "The House That Ruth Built" T-shirts (adults to double-X)
- Commemorative T-shirts (World Series, opening day, retired player day, etc.; usually adults only to double-X)
- "Property of the Yankees" sweatshirts (children and adults)
- "Batting T" style sweatshirts (children and adults)
- Pennants (too many styles to mention, which also tended to get ruined in transit, and the sticks were a pain in the…)
- Visiting team pennants (years ago, we would be given a few pennants of the visiting team; now, they don't sell, so they went bye-bye)
- Inflatable baseball bats (approximately four feet in length)

- Inflatable baseballs (approximately twelve inches in diameter)
- Soft, cushy baseballs for very young children
- Soft, cushy baseballs with matching small glove for children under three years old
- Twelve-inch wooden baseball bats (they make a great weapon in parts of the South Bronx, so they were ultimately banned in the bleachers)
- Ballpoint pens in the shape of a blue, eight-inch wooden bat
- Ballpoint pens with the Yankee logo on them
- Long pencils with the Yankee logo on them
- Yankee Stadium postcards
- Bumper stickers with the Yankee logo on it
- Small Yankee decals
- Various collectable pins (at least twenty varieties, with different ones every year, including small numbers commemorating retired players-starts with 1, 3, 4, 5, 7, 8, 9, 10 and continuing on up; a visit to monument park before the game would reveal whose number was whose)

Every item mentioned above had to be accounted for at the end of a homestand. That's why, after years of having my own stand, I said goodbye to souvenirs. I loved the fans and I loved the extra money I used to earn, but inventory was the deal breaker. And with all these different items, fans still asked for things I didn't have.

"Do you have Yankee dog tags?"

"Do you have Yankee cufflinks?"

"Do you have golf balls with the Yankee logo on it?"

"Do you have the Yankee thing with the blue thing and Jeter's face on it?"

It's funny now, but on the Yankee website, all of these items are available, including "the thing with the thing; please specify blue or white when ordering." The last time I checked, the leash, collar, and ID-tag set was $29.95.

Fans yearn for what seems like everything, including fandom forever. Some years ago, a friend of mine posed the idea of having his cousin's ashes spread on the field and could I somehow make that happen? His cousin had been a lifelong Yankee fan, and this would be the ultimate sendoff for him. By "make that happen," he meant for me to come to a game early and, *Shawshank Redemption* prison-yard style, drop his cousin's ashes down my pants leg, and onto the field.

That episode never came to fruition, but I have read that being buried in a casket festooned with Yankee logos *can* be arranged. And an urn with your favorite team's interlocking N-Y printed on it can be done for $699. Call yourself a devoted fan? How about being a fan for all of *eternity?*

I think the phrase "one size fits all" is a souvenir salesman's favorite slogan, since it tends to make life a lot easier. It's a terrific catchphrase for hats that have snaps, Velcro, or elastic bands on the back that make them adjustable. When I would pitch this line to potential customers, I would often whisper to myself, "One size fits none… properly" or "No size fits all," but it did in fact work for caps, ponchos, and batting helmets. And it does happen to be true, unless, of course, the customer is morbidly obese, extremely petite, or has an extraordinarily humongous head.

Another favorite line at the stand is the term "it's a collectable." I never quite understood this phrase, because if someone is willing, **anything** is a collectable. When you've gone into a friend's basement or a distant relative's den, one might recall having come across a collection of matchbook covers, thimbles, ashtrays, or coasters from around the world, milk pitchers, small turtle figurines… Anything! Heck, I even have an assortment of Yankee playoff shot glasses, now that I think about it. They're collectables, so "I *collected* 'em."

"One man's junk is another man's collectable," I say. That's why, for a souvenir vendor, "It's a collectable," and "one size fits all" are terrific selling tools.

Manning my souvenir stand

One souvenir vendor was always on the make for a sale. If he ran out of a particular size, his strategy was simple: tell the people what they wanted to hear. When it came to cotton T-shirts, if he only had large and they wanted small, he would say, "It's cotton. It shrinks." If he only had medium and they wondered if they might need large, he'd show them the tag under the collar and claim, "Look—they're pre-shrunk." If he only had extra-large and they were buying for their niece back in Missouri, he'd state, "The kids like to wear 'em baggy nowadays." And if he only had small, he'd change his line to, "The girls like 'em snug—shows off the figure." And the tourists would thank him for the advice every time.

Another vendor would always gripe because his stand happened to be right near a loudspeaker and that loudspeaker was always set to the Yankee radio network and their longtime announcer, John Sterling.

Many Yankee fans love John Sterling, he of the idiosyncratic voice, who broadcasts with bombast using affectionate terms for all of the Yankee regulars. He can be very entertaining with his call, "The-uh-uh-uh-uh…Ya-Ya-Ya—YANKEES Win!" at the end of a game. But listening to him every day can certainly take its toll on employees, who get no reprieve from his rah-rah.

Often, around mid-season, this vendor would threaten to cut the wire of the speaker. "I'm gonna do it. I swear I'm gonna do it." Well, eventually he did; one Sunday morning, before the gates opened, when no security guards were around to catch him. His stand was a heck of a lot quieter for the rest of that season and boy was I relieved. Oops. I mean… *he* was.

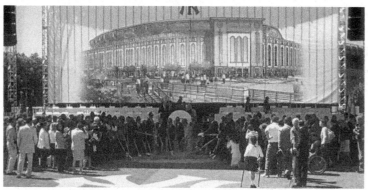

Breaking ground for the new stadium in 2006

When I had a stand, I loved to schmooze with the fans. There's one kid who attended many games who used crutches, because he only had one leg. On his good foot, he sometimes wore a roller skate and scooted around the stands, with his dad always nearby. The two of them were part of the Yankee extended family, and they were even invited to the groundbreaking of the new stadium in 2006.

One time, I remember them at my stand, and the dad wanted to buy him a new Yankee hat to replace his old one. The kid insisted he didn't need it. I loved that kid.

I would often get some strange questions at the stand. A man and his son came up to me once and asked to see an autographed ball. The man looked at it very closely as his eight-year-old son stood by with excitement.

Then the dad asked me, "Are these autographs real? Or repercussions?"

Another time, a lady asked if the shirts only came in "kids' and adults' sizes." I had to think about that one for a second, but I couldn't come up with any response, although I have had many people ask if I had Yankee shirts for their dogs.

Fans sometimes call pennants "pendants" and pins "pennants." One told me his favorite player of all time was Mickey Maris. Somebody even called a rain poncho a "taco."

Now, don't get me wrong: I love language and am fascinated how it can be beautifully mangled. My mother used to call people from the Bahamas "Bohemians," so I am very familiar with the art of malapropisms. It was always fun overhearing fans talk about how Derek Jeter was a big shot, going out to all the Manhattan hot spots with his "entrepenage."

I know I can be a wise guy, but sometimes coping with some of the fans can get rather trying, though it was fun most of the time, that's for sure. A guy came up to my stand one time and asked how much a Yankee hat was. I said, "$21.75."

He said, "I only have $20."

I waited. He waited. I waited some more. He waited some more. Finally I said, "Are you gonna go get some more money? Or is this love?"

Very often, day campers on field trips would come up to me with a handful of change, looking for "anything that cost no more than... *um*, a dollar forty-six." And it was so satisfying when lifelong fans, often middle-aged or older, would make their first visit to the stadium after having spent decades seeing the great shrine only on television.

When a dad was licking an ice cream cone and staring out at the field, I would always laugh when his impatient little son would tug at his leg and say, "Geez, c'mon, Dad. Let's go find our seats."

With experience, I grew shrewd enough to know what items to hide in my inventory box. I may have been allotted some Yankee blankets at the beginning of the season, which obviously didn't sell in June, July, and August, but it was a good idea to have some for September, when the temperature dipped. If I hadn't stashed some and the other stands started calling in after Labor Day to get a delivery for more of them, I might very well have been shut out.

Some items simply didn't sell and I hid them for that reason—*they just didn't sell.* I would move them around the stand so they were displayed more prominently, putting them right in front of the fans' noses, but some items simply didn't sell... *period.* Take, for example, corduroy hats, the kind that are too hot to wear in the summer and too flimsy and cheaply made to be of any value in the cooler autumn and winter months. Whenever I was allocated corduroy hats on opening day, I would bury them in my box and not pull them out again until the season was over, to be returned with my final inventory. For me, Yankee corduroy hats were absolutely useless.

I always thought it was a good idea to start hording retired-player pins of Mickey Mantle and Thurman Munson, so I would have enough for old-timer's day, when those pins were likely to be in demand. If I waited until the last minute, I might lose out again.

Likewise, I would always keep a few cases of ponchos hidden, so, on the drizzly day, when they were needed, I would have them. I would hold them for months at a time, but when it started to pour and I called down to the souvenir room for more, they had often ran out of them. When it comes to ponchos, it's always a good idea to "*a-hum,* save 'em for a rainy day."

Yankee Stadium always drew groups: busloads of Little Leaguers, Greek-Americans, Veterans of War, New Englanders,

Canadians, Brooklyn women's clubs, and so many others, giving me an opportunity to meet and know a varied clientele. In recent years, with the Yankees signing players from different countries (Japan, China, Korea, etc.), we would get fans from all around the world cheering on who, to them, was their local hero. Before the Yankees signed him, Ichiro Suzuki had his most effective seasons with Seattle, and he was undoubtedly the Mariners' best player. Often the Japanese community would buy out the whole section where Ichiro would be playing—usually left field—and there would be a sea of Asian people in those stands, helping the game become truly international.

Boink! No wonder the Yanks never signed me

Often, these tourists from Asia were great souvenir customers, purchasing as many as six to a dozen T-shirts to bring back home to Japan. During some of those years, the Yankees had a terrific All-Star outfielder named Hideki Matsui, and his T-shirt was extremely popular. By the way, "thank you" in Japanese is "ah-ree-got-toh."

One game, two sweet Japanese women came up to my stand and were doing a little shopping. Working on commission and dealing directly with the public, I took extreme care in how I treated my customers. These women were very specific in what they wanted and, most importantly for me, how much they wanted to spend.

After about five minutes of assisting them with their broken English and placing a number of various-sized shirts in plastic bags, I was "this close" to making a sale of well over a hundred dollars, a nice sale on any day. But just as I was closing the deal, another woman strolled up to my stand from the opposite direction. This woman was an unassuming, overweight midwesterner in her forties, who happened to be wearing a T-shirt of her own, though this T-shirt was not a Yankee shirt.

Oh no! This t-shirt happened to have written emblazoned across the front,

PEARL HARBOR

So that's the scenario. I'm about to finish my sale with the two lovely Japanese women and collect my money just as I'm trying to keep this other woman and her commemorative shirt out of their view. While I was chatting with the two Japanese women, I angled myself toward the other woman, speaking to her almost in profile over my shoulder and doing whatever I could to get her the hell out of there.

Thankfully, it all worked out. The big sale was made to the two women ("ah-ree-got-toh"), the mid-westerner left and came back later in the game to buy a doll, and I made my commission. In trying times, a slight pivot of the foot is sometimes all that is needed.

Since the new ballpark opened in 2009, a company worked in conjunction with the Yankees to sell off virtually any remnants from the old stadium. One can purchase "Authentic Yankee Freeze-Dried Grass Sod," advertised as "the most sacred turf in all of sports," complete with the requisite Letter of Authenticity.

When the old stadium was closing down for renovations in 1974-75, I was able to walk out of the ballpark with a seat from the final game of 1973, which I lugged home on the subway. For some inexplicable reason, I gave it to my brother-in-law, and it now sits in his basement, even though he is a devoted Mets fan.

When the old Madison Square Garden closed its doors in 1968, I managed to get out of there with a wooden armrest from a seat, as well. I'm not sure where that ended up. But absconding with artifacts is now a big business, so, if one wants to have a pair of seats from the original Yankee Stadium (with a Letter of Authenticity, of course), they can be had, last time I checked, for the bargain price of $1,499.

It's been a while since I sold my autographed baseballs with "repercussions," but perhaps I should have stayed in the souvenir department instead of switching over to "Beer Here." The president of the memorabilia company hawking the old items made some good points when he said:

"This is not just another stadium that's going down and a new one put up. What happens to this stadium is a very emotional issue to a lot of people. What keeps me up at night is knowing that there are so many folks who want to get something—something they feel good about, something they can afford."

Yes. And since some tickets are now actually $1500 to watch a game... *one game* (if I paid that much for tickets, that would keep *me* up at night)..., maybe $1,499 is a bargain for two original stadium seats that can actually be taken home... and sat in *forever*.

When I sold souvenirs from my booth, I was able to appreciate the fans much more than by simply selling them food in the stands. If someone wanted to buy a beer, that was usually all they needed. They made the transaction and, in a matter of seconds, went on their way with little desire to chat. My relationship with them was similar to a toll collector with a motorist—short and sweet.

Souvenir customers, on the other hand, loved to talk. They would look at a poster or baseball card and tell me a story about their favorite player. Many times, they would linger for an inning or more, and I would play the role of bartender to their quiet, lonely customer persona. I would hear about when they saw a particular favorite of theirs flag down a cab in Manhattan, or when another player was especially nice to their son or daughter. As a salesman, I would often convince them that a sweatshirt looked great when they were indecisive, but I also talked them out of something, if I got the sense they really didn't need it, or couldn't afford it.

There were times when fans would literally cry at my stand, sharing tales of long ago, when their fathers played catch with them in the backyard, or wishing, "Pop lived long enough to come see the stadium." Many told me of how they had turned down a much-needed part-time job because they wanted to play baseball, going to their high school varsity team's practices when they could have, and perhaps *should* have, been working and earning money. They simply had a "love of the game," and I felt privileged to have been confided in with their memories.

I rarely had that kind of intimacy from the fans in the seats who needed a hot dog or a beer. They seemed to be more fixated on the action on the field rather than tell me anecdotes of their childhood. But hanging out near Main 19 through long rain delays, meeting people from far-off places I'd never been to, like… Georgia, for instance, and talking to a grandmother from Wisconsin who brought two grandkids along with her to the Bronx—now *that* was special. It truly was.

THE BALANCING ACT

WE ALL SEEM TO strive for balance in our lives. How can we fulfill our needs, be they financial, creative, or both, and still maintain stability? It's not easy.

My dad's balancing act, once he got out of the vending business as a teenager, was driving a cab, working in his father's butcher shop, and then going to night school at Fordham University to learn the insurance business. Later, he would become a salesman to help put his four kids through college.

My balancing act was my vending job at Yankee Stadium and my career as an actor. In 1977, I attended acting school in Manhattan for three years after graduating from Lehman College in the Bronx, and from 1980 until I left the stadium, I worked around the Yankee schedule to get to my auditions. Sometimes, I would show up at the ballpark wearing a suit and tie and fellow vendors would say, "Had an audition today, huh Stew?"

In fact, many of the vendors pulled for me to get my big break, primarily because they knew, if I got a TV series or a large part in a movie, I might not return to my vending job, thus moving this avaricious lot up on the all-important seniority list. In show business, people working in commercials want to be on a TV show, and those on a TV show want a movie career. In the ballpark the peanut man dreams of hot dogs, while the hot dog guy would love to be selling beer. Is that art imitating life or vice versa?

Fortunately for me, most weekday games took place at night. I would tend to have an audition during the day, so I rarely had any conflicts; especially since audition times are often flexible, leaving a large window of time for the meeting. In July and August, some day games were occasionally during the week and were added to accommodate summer camps, but those were the exception to the rule. It's when I got a callback, the second round of auditions when the acting job is closer to becoming a reality, that there was virtually no wiggle room for my appointment time, and I often had to sacrifice a game. When my agent told me I had a callback for Toyota at 4:40 p.m., I had better be there at 4:40, or I would have no chance of booking that job.

Another aspect of callbacks is actors tend to wear the exact same clothing they wore to the initial audition. I always keep notes to remember what I wore, who I met, etc. I still have the tweed jacket I was wearing when I booked three episodes of *Columbo*, while living in Los Angeles. I hope there are a few more detective jobs for me still left in that coat.

Days of callbacks were pure speculation, when I gambled giving up the sure money of a game on the possibility I would book the acting job and make even more money, or perhaps advance my acting career with a prestigious role. Since auditions and acting gigs can sometimes be sparse over a long period of time, the security of my Yankee job all those years was a comfort on the first of every month, when my rent was due. Then again, balancing my appointments often got a bit hectic. One week, I auditioned for roles as a janitor, attorney, mafia boss, policeman, and a bicycle rider with hemorrhoids for a Preparation H commercial, all in the midst of a busy homestand.

My balancing act meant that sometimes I received last-minute calls at the most inopportune times. A few years ago, I went to Richmond, Virginia to meet up with a friend for a few days. The day before, I had had my third callback for a part in a Broadway show, and this was to be a brief but welcome summer holiday, while the Yankees were on the road. We had plans for a barbeque—Chesapeake crabs—golf, and lots of fun and relaxation. Since another friend was staying in the area, the strategy was for the two of them to meet me at the train station for dinner, and then we'd take the hour and a half drive through backcountry to my buddy's place.

However, sometime between Baltimore and Washington, my cell phone rang. It was my agent. Apparently, the playwright had loved my audition the previous day, but now the director wanted to see me. "Tomorrow morning at 11:10."

Usually, I am thrilled to get callbacks. In this case, it was extra special, since I'd never done a play on Broadway before. But on this particular day, I was on a train to Richmond with golf clubs in tow.

I told my agent I would call her back in an hour and think it over. When I got off that Amtrak train in Richmond, I told my friends I had good news and bad news. And so, after taking a six-hour ride to meet them, we walked across the street to a bar, had a beer and some limp mozzarella sticks, and then I took the very next train back to Penn Station in New York. I had spent a grand total of fifty minutes in Richmond. And not only did I travel thirteen hours that day, I had to pay $125 for my round-trip ticket, as well.

Sometimes, it can take more than twenty different auditions to book a job. They rarely come easily, so I wasn't surprised that all my anxiety was for nothing, since, the next day, the director was so rude, she actually was *knitting* during my reading.

I had heard horror stories about auditions from friends for years, but this time I was pissed and tempted to say, "Excuse me, Mrs. Huckenfutz. I am about to do something very interesting here with my face—a very comical look, where my forehead gets all wrinkly and expressive. If you don't glance up from that baby blanket you are working on, you are going to miss seeing a strong clue to understanding the raw soul of my character..."

But I held my tongue. Actually, in the excitement and stress of the moment of the callback, I was mostly focusing on my

work. It was only when I finished up and was heading home on the subway did I feel frustrated by this woman's rude behavior. Oh, and "P.S.," as my mother used to say, I *didn't* get the part.

My day job... unless it was a night game

I was in California one year when my agent called to say she'd managed to get me an interview with famed director Sidney Lumet for an upcoming movie. Since he'd directed *Serpico, Network,* and *12 Angry Men* among many others, I cut my LA trip short and flew back to New York to have a meeting with Sidney Lumet. For exactly forty-five seconds. Yup, that's all the time it took for this wonderful director to realize he *didn't* want to cast me in his movie.

Ah, show business—the glamour, the excitement... the unemployment. But hey, it's not everybody who can say, "I met... Sidney Lumet."

As an actor, it's crucial to do and say whatever is necessary to get the job. Once I went on an audition for a Sprite commercial, and I was reading for the part of a Russian hockey player. The casting director asked me if I could ice skate, and I said, "Sure...," quietly continuing to myself, "...Glad she didn't ask if I could *stop*."

A week later, I was booked as an extra and told to meet a van in Manhattan with the other hockey player/actors, to ride to the ice rink out in New Jersey where the commercial was being shot. I was thrilled, and, since I like to be prepared, I brought along some extra sweat socks so, when I put on my skates at the arena, I would be comfortable and, I *thought*, professional.

Riding in that van, listening to the other hockey players chatting, had to be one of the most fearful and awkward hours of my life.

First of all, they each carried huge bags of gear, which included as many as six hockey sticks and various shoulder guards, hip pads, etc. Apparently, most of these guys had played together on local pick-up teams and college varsity squads, so they shared common stories—of concussions, stitches to the face, visits to emergency rooms, and so on. I quietly sat in the back of the van, wincing at each of their reminiscences, and desperately clutching my extra pair of sweat socks, occasionally using them to wipe my panic-stricken brow.

When we got to the location for the shoot, I was almost sick to my stomach with fear. I immediately went to the production assistant in charge of checking us in and told her that, rather than be a "skating" player, I enthusiastically offered to be the goalie, figuring there wouldn't be much skating involved at the net.

Not one of my smartest suggestions, as I soon realized not only did the goalie need to be perhaps the best skater of all, quickly darting forward and back at lightning speed, but he needed to stop a puck flying at his head at a thousand miles an hour.

I went into the locker room to put on equipment that had

been laid out for me. We were to be a Russian hockey team who, at some point in the commercial, would skate over to the camera and hold up cans of Sprite while yelling out, "Sprites-ky" or something like that.

"Sprites-ky" I could do. But getting into a hockey uniform was a completely different matter. Frankly, I had never put on hip guards or giant suspenders before, and, by the way, goalie pads are absolutely *enormous*. As the guys were joking around in the locker room, casually putting on their equipment as if they were slipping into pajamas, I was struggling not to look like the idiot I truly was. A quiet, sobering conversation was slowly formulating between my ears.

> Stew. Go to the production assistant. Tell her you can't skate. Tell her you are very sorry and you would be more than happy to take a bus back to the city... Or even walk back through the Lincoln Tunnel, if necessary, and pretend this day never happened. Do it, Stew. There will be more auditions, more jobs. Live another day, buddy.

But I *didn't* listen to myself. I somehow put on all the equipment, furtively watching my colleagues, mimicking their moves every step of the way, quietly whimpering to myself as I did. I then went from the locker room to the ice rink and warmed up by unsteadily skating ten feet and then clutching the sideboards for dear life for the next ten feet.

Fortunately for me it wasn't long before the commercial's director realized I couldn't skate at all (Hey, I could skate. They just didn't ask me if I could *stop*), so they told me to take off all the goalie equipment. They now wanted me to be one of the players who were seated on the bench. This turned out to be the best news of the day, as I kept my extra pair of sweat socks on, took off the skates (thank God), and learned a bitter lesson in survival. Plain and simple, if an actor at an audition says they can skate, they better know how to skate. And oh yeah, that goes for lion taming, as well.

One spring, my girlfriend and I had plans to go to Europe, but I had a callback the week before for a national commercial, which can be a very lucrative job. Of course, the commercial was to be shot the same days we were to be in Italy, but since the payout was potentially quite large, I told my agents we would cancel the trip if I got the part. My gal knew the idiosyncrasies of my business, and we bought travel insurance just in case.

Unfortunately, producers tend to keep actors in suspense by not making their final decisions until the very last moment. It's not intentional; they can be more insecure about their work than actors. So I didn't find out for sure that I was released from the job until we were two thirds of the way to the airport. At least that was a win/win scenario, since the consolation prize was going to Europe for ten days, but it was an extremely stressful way to pack our luggage, that's for sure. I did get to call out "Beer Here" to an empty Roman Coliseum, so that was another fun consolation for me.

Once, when I was living in Los Angeles, I actually had an acting job but couldn't get to the set on time. That was frustrating.

The job was for a Monday, but I had to fly to Florida for my uncle's funeral that weekend. I was due at Universal Studios in LA at 10 a.m. on the Monday for some cop show, but my return flight out of Miami on Sunday night made a connection out of Atlanta that was cancelled due to rain, so I had to fly out early the following morning.

The airline put me up in a hotel near the airport in Atlanta and my flight was scheduled to leave at 9 a.m. East Coast time. With the time difference, it would get me to LA around 11:30 a.m. Pacific time. I didn't sleep well that night, partly because I was possibly going to be missing out on a day's acting job, and also because, by staying near the airport, I heard airplanes taking off all night and into the morning. I sat up in bed wondering, "How come I'm not on *that* plane?"

When I called the studio from my room on the Monday

morning, it was three hours earlier on the West Coast. I had to leave a longwinded message on an answering machine in the middle of the night, stating I wouldn't be able to make my call time and was so very sorry, it was beyond my control, blah-blabbity-blah.

Once I landed in Los Angeles, I called again, and, of course, the office was furious I couldn't get to the set on time. They were forced to recast the role at the last minute. My agent told me I never should have gone to the funeral, putting his agency's standing in jeopardy with the casting director.

Losing the job was frustrating, but getting scolded by my agent was worse, since I ended up feeling guilty about going to my uncle's funeral. They hadn't hired me for the weekend, only the Monday, but that's part of the balancing act—trying to stay sane when the whole neighborhood is having a conniption.

I've grown to realize, no matter how nervous I can be at an audition, the production company making the decision about me is even more nervous. They have a big budget at stake (or a *little* budget, which can be even more unnerving), and they have a lot more riding on whether or not I get cast than even I do.

As a union vendor at the old stadium, I was entitled to sign up for work the day prior to a game, allowing me to come to the ballpark an hour later than non-union vendors. That hour proved very valuable to me as I balanced my auditions, rehearsals, and tapings with the vagaries of the Yankee schedule. The new stadium has a completely different protocol for signing in, but the old method brought with it some balancing-act stress. By signing in, I was declaring to the vending company I would be there on time. Unless I phoned them with sufficient notice to say I wouldn't be able to make it in that day, if I didn't show up, I was docked from work for the next three scheduled games, resulting in a large loss of revenue.

One day, I helped a buddy out by driving his car to his apartment. He, too, was an actor, and he had an audition, so he asked me to do him this favor. *No problem*, I thought, as, even though I had a night game, I figured I had plenty of time to pick up his car on the East Side, take it over to the West Side, double park, hike up the stairs to his fourth-floor apartment, drop off a duffle bag full of his clothes, and return his car to him prior to getting up to the Bronx for my game.

When I arrived at his building on 47th Street and Eleventh Avenue, I had to double-park, as I had expected to do. I lugged the duffle bag up the stairs and, once I got there, had a little problem with the lock on his door, jimmying the key back and forth. I noticed a neighbor looking out the window down the hallway, a white-haired little old Irish lady.

"Do you have a blue Pinto?" she asked.

"Yes," I said.

"Well," she replied in her delicate, crisp brogue, "looks like you're getting a ticket."

Boom! I went flying down the stairs, leaving his key in the lock and his duffle bag on the ground. When I got to the car, sure enough, I had a ticket. I also had a problem, because my buddy's key was stuck in the lock and his duffel bag was sitting in his hallway, so I climbed back up the stairs and tried to tackle my little dilemma. Those old buildings on the West Side never have an elevator when necessary; "pre-war" is the quaint term, I believe.

After a few moments of jiggling, the key was permanently lodged in the lock. Then the neighbor, still looking out the window, turned to me and said with that lovely Irish twinkle, "Now it looks like you're getting towed."

Aggh! I went flying down the stairs again, just in time to see my friend's blue Pinto getting hauled down the block, hooked up to one of New York's finest tow trucks. So, nothing to do but go upstairs and try dealing with the key, which was jammed even further into the lock.

Of course, time was now becoming a factor for me. The next thing I knew, I was roaming the West Side searching for a telephone (PCP—pre-cell phone), to call my friend to give him the news: his car was towed, his key was stuck in his door, and I was roaming the West Side of Manhattan dragging his clothes around like they were a huge dead carcass. Plus, I had to get to my game.

Thankfully, this friend is a good-natured soul. He raced over, calling in late for his waiter's shift, summoned a locksmith, left his clothes with another neighbor (I think the Irish lady went in for her afternoon nap), and started the process of bailing out his towed car while I headed off to the Bronx and my Yankee night game.

Most people are aware of the difficulties of surviving in the arts. When I first started making the rounds of theatrical agents' offices, I was shocked by some of the things I saw; the sheer volume of competition I ran into.

One time, I dropped off my picture and résumé at an agent's office, and, after I knocked on the door and was told to come in, I saw a rather obese woman in a light-blue chiffon dress lying on a couch. She was in repose, reading *The New York Times*, while navigating a bacon, lettuce, and tomato sandwich, which was sitting on a plate, balanced perfectly on her stomach. From under that mountain of newspaper and fat, I heard her say, "Just put your picture on that stack over there, sweetie," as she pointed to a large pile of manila envelopes.

I cautiously did as I was told and quietly headed out the door. A business encounter such as this was never mentioned in acting school, and the image of that heaving woman still haunts me to this day.

My very first job on television was as an extra on a soap opera called *Search for Tomorrow*. My part was so small, the show could have been called *Search for Stewart*.

I, of course, alerted my family that I was to be on, and one of my sisters later told me how she had witnessed my television debut. She had been playing cards with her friends that day, and, since this was before videotaping, DVRs, and all the rest, she made her friends stop the game in anticipation of her baby brother being on his first television show. I didn't appear until the end of the episode, so that didn't go over too well with the card players.

My part called for me to be in an elevator with some other extras while the principal actors (those who actually had lines to say) were performing their scene. Eventually, the elevator door opened up, my sister screamed *"THERE HE IS!"* the principals stepped out and started talking, the elevator door closed, and my sister sputtered to her friends, "...*AND*...there...he...goes!"

One other extra job I did was in Woody Allen's film *Zelig*. I was to portray a townsperson attending a Hitler rally in 1940s Germany. What fun for a nice Jewish boy, pretending to cheer on Hitler.

Anyway, in the holding area where the extras hung out until called to the set, there were many civilians for the scene but also many others dressed as German soldiers. All of us were essential for the elaborate political rally that Allen had concocted. What I found fascinating was, in the holding area, the townspeople stuck with the townspeople and the Nazis stuck with the Nazis. It made sense, since each of the groups was called to the set together, so they gravitated toward one another as they were hanging out.

While waiting, I could see across the way the actors who were portraying Nazis, biding their time by playing poker. It struck me how intimidated and scared of them I was. Their uniforms, coupled with their Aryan looks, which had helped get them cast, made me fearful of even walking over to their side of the room. A lesson in the power of a costume, that's for sure.

Before I got involved in the business, I didn't have much of a clue as to what it takes to get an acting job, *any* acting job. When I was in Los Angeles in the early nineties, I was thrilled to be booked on a fried chicken commercial. Commercials for fast food can be quite remunerative, since they can appear during any television program, any time of day, any time of year, and the residuals can mount from such exposure. I was also excited about this particular job, because I have a weakness for fried chicken. I couldn't imagine anything better: getting paid to eat chicken, one of my true loves.

I was booked for two days of chicken eating. When I got to the set, they had supplied me and the other actors, those playing my wife and two children, with "spit buckets." Once the camera panned away, these buckets were to be used to spit the chicken out. No need to continue eating when the camera wasn't on me, since I was going to be eating chicken for numerous takes.

To me, this was absurd. I wasn't going to spit any chicken out—I loved this product, and so I ate it all day. Day one, I devoured eight delicious breasts; the director and the crew couldn't believe it. Day two, I couldn't eat a bite. I was so nauseous throughout the rest of the shoot, I actually feared I might never have the taste for fried chicken again. What had been my dream job, eating fried chicken and getting paid for it, had quickly turned into my worst nightmare.

I remember one shot in particular. My "commercial" family was seated around the kitchen table, while the director was on a camera dolly, circling behind them as he filmed a close-up on me. Since there was no dialogue involved, he was able to talk to me while he was shooting.

He would say, "Okay, smile at your wife. Good. Now look over to your son. Nice. Now the girl. Excellent."

What was strange was that, the whole time he was talking to me, asking me to smile, and telling me to show my love for my kids and wife, these make-believe family members of mine were each spitting chicken into their buckets. The camera wasn't on them, so they could do that while I, on camera, was beaming, watching my loved ones heaving at the dinner table. Ah, show business—the glamour, the excitement... the nauseated.

I have been fortunate to do theater, film, and television, directing and teaching when the opportunity arises. I helped start a theater company in the standard New York way, selling assorted donated items from our members on a street on the Lower East Side to raise cash. With the $100 or so we raised, we purchased stationery to then ask for more funding from relatives and friends to actually do a production. It's the best way to get off the ground and, I believe, some kind of theatrical tradition.

After I graduated from acting school, my first show was an original play where I was cast as the father of a girl in her late teens. I was only twenty-four, but I was playing someone twice my age, a farmer from Kansas, so I grew a beard, put gray in my hair, worked on an accent, and *kinda* pulled it off... I think. At least I thought so at the time.

At the end of the first act, I had a scene with the girl who played my daughter where she was to tell me she didn't want to go into the family business, had an urge to attend college instead, and, in fact, was thinking of moving to big bad New York City to go to art school. It was a very intense and emotional scene, but, one performance, as it got more and more heated, I could see from the look in the girl's eyes that she was in that "nowhere" zone, completely at a loss for her next line. Panic was lurking as the scene's momentum dropped, and there was a long pause that had never been there before.

Fortunately, and I still don't know how it happened, I was able to improvise, quickly seeing the pages of the script and her lines in my head. After what seemed like a thirty-second black hole of silence, I said to her, "I suppose the next thing you're going to tell me is you want to go to art school in New York."

She immediately woke from the zone with a wide-eyed look and blurted out, "*Yes. Yes!* That's *exactly* what I was going to say!"

One spring, I was invited onto a talk show to discuss a play I was starring in. It was an off-Broadway play called *The Mugger*, about a man out for revenge, in which I played the title role. The talk show was *The Joe Franklin Show*.

Joe Franklin was a radio and television institution in New York City, known as "The King of Nostalgia," preserving all things related to entertainment as he took his listeners and viewers down his self-proclaimed "Memory Lane." He promoted every form of show business and was a pioneer for talk show hosts. Over the course of his career, he interviewed celebrities from Marilyn Monroe to Charlie Chaplin, John Lennon to Bob Hope, and Salvador Dalí to Barbra Streisand. On the other hand, he also presented some under-rehearsed animal trainers, clumsy jugglers, and ventriloquists who spoke with a lisp, all of whom would have had a difficult time finding work anywhere. Billy Crystal, when he was a regular on *Saturday Night Live*, parodied Franklin perfectly, and I, in the early stages of my show business life, was thrilled to be able to sit and schmooze on Joe's couch.

The play I was in wasn't very good and actually closed in a week—rightly so—but being on Franklin's show was an experience I won't forget. His desk was a sloppy mess, strewn with press releases, photos, press kits, and the like. I brought a few publicity shots from *The Mugger* for him to display during my appearance. However, once the taping was over and I went to get the pictures back, they had been swallowed up on his disheveled heap of a desk. He had shuffled everything around during the time I was there, and I had to help him search for the pictures to return to our theater's marquee, since they were our production's only photos. I think I found them underneath some promotional stills of a Lebanese belly dancer who worked with a chimpanzee as her assistant. And the funny thing is... I'm not kidding.

There were two other guests on the couch for my show: a woman who self-published some cheesy novels one might buy at a supermarket checkout counter, and a man dressed in a tuxedo. He was an entertainer *of some kind* who apparently did an act at the Valley Forge Inn in the Poconos, on Thursdays at three in the afternoon, where he imitated Dean Martin. His partner, who played Jerry Lewis, should consider himself lucky he was not on Franklin's show. Martin and Lewis, of course, had been big stars back in the fifties and this guy on the couch looked somewhat like Martin, with his deep dark tan. He lip-synched a version of Dean's hit, "Everybody Loves Somebody Sometime." *Lip-synched.* I must admit, it was rather odd sitting next to this orange man in a tuxedo, watching him move his lips to the music.

After my brief interview talking about the lousy play I was in, Joe playfully asked Dino to do an impression of Jerry Lewis. The guy, perplexed and somewhat at a loss for words said, "Uh, no, Joe. I do *Dean*. My **partner** does Jerry."

Franklin giggled and playfully said, "I know you do Dean, but, just for kicks, let me hear you do Jerry."

Dino wouldn't bite. It was truly awkward with a capital "AWK."

I had been able to get on the show in the first place because a cousin of mine worked on the same floor as Franklin in a Times Square building. After standing and chatting at a urinal next to him for about six months, my cousin finally convinced the talk show host to have me on. Later I realized, by appearing on *The Joe Franklin Show* that day, talking about my short-lived off-Broadway debut, I may very well have had the biggest credits of any guest there. Surreal... but true.

There have been many actors who used their job as vendors to help support themselves as they sought fame. Years ago, comedian Jimmie "J.J." Walker—who went on to star in the sitcom *Good Times,* immortalizing the phrase "Dy-No-MITE!"—started as a vendor in the Bronx. By the time I retired, there were at least a half dozen actors and comedians who shared audition stories in the locker room before going out to sell their items.

While pursuing my acting career, I have also taught acting at many schools. The old saying, "Those that can...**do,** and those that can't...**teach**," is absurd. I believe that those who can...*should* teach.

One of my most gratifying moments as a teacher was when I had a girl in my class who had Down syndrome. Her mother would accompany her to class for each session. Whenever I taught beginning actors, I would instruct them to do a monologue of their choosing—could be a poem, could be a speech from a movie, could even be a letter; anything that would motivate them to work hard enough so they studied and memorized it. In fact, it didn't even have to be from a person of their gender. They were free to wear a costume, use props—anything that would make them comfortable; the fewer rules and restrictions imposed on them the better. I didn't want them to feel inhibited in any way whatsoever. The key was for the students to be inspired by the work they chose for themselves.

This young girl, who was about eighteen, chose to do a speech from a television movie called *Brian's Song*, based on a true story, starring James Caan and Billy Dee Williams. For her monologue, she chose to play the part of football great Gale Sayers, the black teammate to Brian Piccolo, who had been stricken with a fatal disease. The film had been groundbreaking during the seventies because it shed light on an interracial friendship between two teammates, something rarely dramatized at that time.

The scene called for Sayers, one of the sport's greatest players, to give a speech at a testimonial dinner. He was receiving a trophy, and, rather than do a gratuitous acceptance speech, he chose to speak of his dear friend Brian, who, at that moment, was gravely ill in a hospital.

It's a moving exhortation, and this girl, who happened to be white, came in wearing a tuxedo and an Afro wig for the part of Sayers, which was appropriate for the work. She struggled with her words, partially because of her own illness and partially because she was in character, but it all was so inspiring—this white, eager, mentally challenged teenage girl playing a black, male adult. Her dedication and commitment to the work was stellar. Black. White. Male. Female. Didn't matter. Every one of us in the room that day was holding back tears as she appealed to her audience to pray for her friend Brian.

Since auditioning means repeatedly going on job interviews, booking one is a rewarding feeling. A few years ago, I went through the complete casting process and managed to get hired for a memorable commercial. Getting that job turned out to literally change my life.

The commercial was a clever spot about identity theft. It called for me to sit in a lounge chair in my wood-paneled den while watching a bowling tournament on my television set. When I started to speak, however, my voice was that of a twenty-something "Valley girl," presumably the one who stole my credit card and, thus, my identity. In the ad, I talked about buying "a leather bustier," a ridiculous notion seeing me, a blue-collar beer drinker, sloppy and disheveled, seated in my comfy chair, relaxing.

When I booked the commercial, my agent told me the ad agency hadn't decided on the exact day we would be shooting. "Either Monday or Tuesday," I remember her saying.

After the good news of getting the job sunk in, it dawned on me: "Oh no. The playoffs start Tuesday and the Yanks are home against the Twins." Since I had a souvenir stand that year, I was potentially going to be in a bind.

When I was simply vending beer, I could miss games by calling ahead, but when I had a souvenir stand, I signed on for every single game, no exceptions. Could I take a potentially big acting job and possibly lose my stand during a year that looked like the Yanks would get to the World Series? I thought it over and just figured, "Why worry about something beyond my control?"

Fortunately for me, the call came in telling me the shoot was going to be on the *Monday,* leaving me free to work the Tuesday playoff game as well.

As it turns out, the commercial went on to be very popular. It aired nationally for three years, won an Emmy as the best commercial of 2004, and made me somewhat recognizable for as long as it ran. Fans would often spot me in the stands and say, "Hey! There's the bustier guy!"

I was an official member of the "fifteen minutes of fame" club. Actually, I used to say that in my case it was "fifteen *seconds* of fame," since it was only a commercial. It's still on YouTube, I believe. Perhaps forever.

The truly amazing aspect of the commercial and what

changed my life is that, one day, I came home around the time it was running and had a message on my answering machine. It turned out an old girlfriend of mine had seen the ad and called me to say hello. She was coming to New York from her home in Miami and was wondering if we could get together.

At this time in my life, I was very busy professionally, as the commercial opened up a few modest opportunities for me in film and television. In addition, I was just getting ready to perform in a new play in New York. Yet, even though I was seeing some success with my career, my love life was at its lowest. I was single, but I wasn't exactly a *swinging* single. I had been casually dating a Russian girl, but it was going nowhere, and I often referred to her to my friends as "Elena Yakantsleepova."

My identity theft commercial

Back in the late seventies, there was a very beautiful girl at Yankee Stadium who sold popcorn. Her father had been the attorney of one of George Steinbrenner's secretaries, and he was able to pull some strings to get his daughter a job at the ballpark. When we first met, she was seventeen and I was twenty-one; after a few little flirtations, we were officially an item. We ended up being together for two years, but I went to acting school and we later broke up. The old story: too young to realize what a beautiful thing we had.

In the years since we parted, I had thought about this girl... a lot. She was the proverbial "one that got away." She had distinctive, blonde curly locks á la Shirley Temple or Little Orphan Annie, and soft, angelic skin. But she was also tough. One game, her money bag was stolen from her stand, and she chased the perpetrator through the hallway into the seats and grabbed him. Fortunately, some cops were there in time, as the thief was about to hit her on the back of her head with the butt of his gun. How he got a gun into Yankee Stadium, I don't know. On hearing about this incident, her boss was shocked she had gone to such an extreme to save the company's money. He admitted to me that even *he* would have let the guy go rather than run him down.

This girl and I had great fun together in the late-seventies, taking out-of-town trips and having unique experiences as youthful lovers. Needless to say, she was the girl who called me up after seeing the identity theft commercial. Unfortunately, when I replayed her phone message, *aaggh*! I couldn't make out her number. It was a bit garbled, and I couldn't tell if those last four numbers were "fifteen-oh-three" or "fifteen-oh-eight." Or "*six*teen-oh-eight?" I replayed her message over and over and jotted down onto a pad the combinations I thought it might possibly be. Soon, I was staring at a sheet of paper with eight telephone numbers and praying one of them was Sharon's, the girl I had been spending twenty-four years trying to *forget*, to help ease the pain of missing her.

So, scribbled right in front of me was the key to unlocking my happiness, a possible chance to see her again and... who knows? I anxiously waited for the right moment. I was nervous. It was actually the first time I ever took a shower to make a phone call.

I started dialing. Strike one. Strike two. Strike three. Strike four. Remember, I had eight strikes. And then... *Bingo*! She had moved to Miami to start a gourmet food business and was flying to New York for a trade show on a day when I was working a Yankee game (what else is new?), but we met up after the game at my apartment, the same apartment we had lived in together many years earlier.

Our meeting was a little uncomfortable at first, since we hadn't seen each other in *twenty-four* years. I was, of course, panicked. She's a gourmet, a foodie, so I ran to the store and got a platter of vegetables with some kind of dippy thing in the middle. *That'll impress her*, I thought. A crudités platter. Yeah, *that'll do it*.

She rang the bell and climbed the flight of stairs she'd used to *hop up* twenty-four years earlier. We had an awkward hug at the door, and I offered her some wine, which she'd been kind enough to bring. I brought out the crudités plate, which she smiled at but never touched. I asked her what she thought of all the changes I'd made to the place in the many years since she'd left, and she said, "Uh... it looks exactly the same." She was right.

However, in relatively no time at all, we were sharing stories of our past, together and apart. In a word, it was wonderful. Afterward, she had a business dinner she was committed to, so I escorted her downtown in a taxi and dropped her off at the restaurant.

When I left her and started to walk back to the subway to come back uptown, I was literally shaking. My life had been rushing before me, and I couldn't believe my good fortune: my long-lost love from twenty-four years ago had come back into my life all because of a commercial. I was so discombobulated I bumped into a fence and almost fell to the ground. People came up to me in the street to see if I was okay, wondering if I was drunk or even sick. In the ensuing days, when I spoke to her on the phone, I told her how glad I was that she hadn't called me while I was still married to my first wife, since that would have completely broken my heart.

Since I was in rehearsals for a play and the Yankees were in the midst of a long homestand, I didn't have much free time.

About a week after we met up after all those years, I had one day off—my only day off for the next three weeks. So I told her I was coming down to Miami, even if it was only for a single Thursday. Actually, I was there for nineteen hours, but I was not going to miss out on this opportunity; I was not going to let her forget me.

Well, she didn't... And, six years later to the day of the anniversary of that meeting, we got married. We will happily grow old together, "in thickness and in health," as I like to say. My friends are still amazed she called after seeing me in *that* commercial, where I frankly looked the picture of sloppiness, but she did.

Sharon with our loving dog, Lucee

She now teaches me how to live right and love right, all the time. She is a great friend of orphaned animals—which is a true barometer of a person's character—always finding the time to pet, or even adopt, a stray dog or cat. And, like my mom did years earlier, she loves and abuses the English language, which she sometimes finds "problemsome."

I've heard her call text messaging "tex mex," and she once

referred to the singers Captain & Tennille as Tatum O'Neal. I emailed her about the correct spelling for a word, and she wrote back, "Don't ask a dyslexic how to spell," signing the note, "olo." When she says *Dog Day Afternoon* stars Cappuccino, I know just what she means, and I'm sure, if Al Pacino heard that, he would smile just as much as I do.

Baseball and the Yankees helped make all of that good fortune come to me, as the playoffs started on the Tuesday, the identity theft commercial shot on the Monday, and I managed to play the balancing act just right for a change.

THE SIXTIES

THE OLD YANKEE STADIUM, not the new one, was the ultimate ballpark in America. I know fans in Boston scream for Fenway Park, which is a beauty, and those in Chicago claim there is no place like Wrigley Field and they would be right. But even though I am biased because I was born in the Bronx and was a vendor for forty years, the ultimate American ballpark was the original Yankee Stadium, pre *and* post refurbishing.

Fenway, built in 1912, is the oldest stadium in all of baseball. It has the feel of a Minor League park, with the fans tightly packed in. Wrigley, built in 1914, has ivy hanging on the outfield walls and is probably the best place of all to watch a game simply because of the enthusiasm of its fans. They waited for over a century for a championship, and they are as dedicated to their team as our bleacher creatures, with a thorough knowledge of the sport.

The old Yankee Stadium, however, witnessed true greatness. The place where twenty-six championships were won, where monuments were actually placed *on* the field out in center field, not far from the back wall's ominous "461 FT." sign, where more Hall of Famers played than anywhere else, where Babe Ruth doffed his cap countless times, where Lou Gehrig claimed he was "the luckiest man on the face of the Earth," where the only perfect game in World Series history took place, and where DiMaggio, Mantle, Mariano Rivera, and Whitey Ford played every one of their career home games. Generations of spectators have experienced a tradition of excellence, and that's why I believe the other two ballparks fall a little short.

Wrigley, Fenway, and Yankee Stadium all have subway stops nearby, offering the urban life, character, and commotion that commuters provide. And, like Wrigley, where fans over the years brought folding chairs to watch games from rooftops across the street from the ballpark, Yankee Stadium in the old days had fans gather on top of apartment buildings above River Avenue, as it was called then, sneaking a peek at their heroes for free. For decades, fans could also be seen on the platform for the downtown side of the 4 train, trying to peer over the bleacher wall to catch any glimpse they could.

When I attended games back in the '60s and '70s, there was a bakery on 161st Street that seemed to tease me into buying some sort of pastry or black-and-white cookie. Each stop on the 4 train had one of these European-style kosher bakeries, where warm onion rolls and large sheets of cake would be on display in the window. Sherbloom's, famous for its brownies, was on 170th Street and the one on 161st Street, as I recall, was simply called K and R. As time passed, a grocery store/deli/donut shop replaced the bakery. During my final years, I would sometimes go up the street to a twenty-four-hour Spanish restaurant that sold, and still does, such items as tripe soup, pig ears, blood pudding, and potato balls. Though none of it sounds kosher to me, it sure tasted good before or after a night game.

When I was a kid, I would stroll through the shops under the el where there were greasy fast-food joints, mom and pop souvenir stores and two now extinct bowling alleys, Stadium Lanes and Ballpark Lanes. I would spend hours in Manny's Baseball Land looking over the player photos protected in plastic sheets and displayed in the souvenir showcases.

Manny's nourished me more than the food places, since I used to have photos of ballplayers plastered on my bedroom walls: one wall devoted to baseball players, another to football, one to hockey, and the fourth wall to basketball. I rarely, if ever, bought any player photos in a store, since I saved money by cutting them out of magazines and Scotch taping them to my walls. As a young fan, I always looked forward to hanging out at Manny's until they would toss me out, staring all day at souvenirs that, years later, I would sell in the ballpark at my own stand.

Just down the street from Manny's, at one of the fast-food places, there was a short, roly-poly middle-aged German grill man who looked like the Monopoly game's "get out of jail free" guy. He would call out to pedestrians with his thick accent, "C'mon boys. Hamburgers, hot frrranks—c'mon boys." I think the franks and burgers were a quarter at the time, and this guy was one of my first images of a real, larger-than-life hustler determined to make a buck.

As a kid, I was a fan of Yogi Berra and Bobby Richardson. We all know about Yogi, but Richardson was a scrappy second baseman in the sixties who was the personification of a singles hitter. In 1960, when I was only five years old, he had the best series of anyone on the team and perhaps the most productive of anyone of all time. Unfortunately for him, it was lost in the shuffle, because Bill Mazeroski hit a dramatic home run in the bottom of the ninth of game seven to win the championship for the Pittsburgh Pirates.

For that whole season, Richardson knocked in only twenty-six runs, but during the World Series of seven games, he set two records: most RBIs in one game (six) and most RBIs for a series (twelve). Later in his career, he set the record for most hits in a series (thirteen). For some reason, he seemed to step up in October, as his lifetime World Series batting average was almost forty points higher than his regular season batting average.

Richardson was a very religious man, which wasn't easy while being on the boozing and bruising Yanks of the time. And he really wasn't that good of a hitter—a dink here and a dink there. Manager Casey Stengel once said of him, "He don't smoke, he don't drink… and he *still* can't hit .250." I don't know why I followed him so much—I guess I'm an underdog guy and Richardson filled the bill.

Yogi Berra, of course, had some great stories attributed to, or about, him. He famously used to say about a midwest town, "It gets late early out there." Or about a restaurant, "Nobody goes there anymore—it's too crowded." When he was asked whether he preferred to be buried or cremated his response was, "Surprise me."

As the story goes, one time he was in Chicago on a road trip during a very hot summer. On this particular day, he was in the team's hotel lobby wearing a white, seersucker suit, the perfect outfit for the sticky, humid weather. The team owner's wife happened to be strolling through the lobby when she saw him and said, "Hi, Yogi. My, you look quite cool and comfortable in that suit in this weather."

Yogi, quick on the trigger, replied, "You don't look so hot yourself."

Those early sixties teams had some great players. My memory is filled with the images of gimpy Mickey Mantle, Roger Maris defying the odds by breaking Babe Ruth's record for most home runs in a season (61 in '61), and Mel Stottlemyre, warming up off to the side of home plate prior to starting a game, the thud of the pitches echoing loudly into the catcher's glove.

One day, I went to see the Yanks play the Washington Senators. After the game, I snuck onto the field and into the visitor's dugout for about six, maybe seven seconds, and then I jumped back into the stands. While I was in the dugout, however, I grabbed a flimsy towel that I'd observed had been used by Frank Howard, a gigantic home run hitter for the Senators. He was six foot seven and used to wag his bat at the plate like it was a toothpick. He was a good player, a four-time All-Star, so I was overjoyed to have one of his sweaty towels.

When I brought it home, however, my mom yelled at me, "What the heck am I gonna do with *that?*" I screamed and fought with her not to wash my Big League towel, and I kept that thing for two years, though it did eventually get washed.

During the World Series of 1967, I was in Hebrew school, studying Haphtarah lessons for my bar mitzvah the following year. The Haphtarah is what a thirteen-year-old boy must read in front of the temple's congregation on the big day, when he is said to "become a man" and welcomed into the Jewish community.

All of my classmates were die-hard baseball fans, and we wanted to find out how the Red Sox, the hated foe of the Yankees, were doing against the Cardinals in the World Series. Back then, the games were played during the day, no night games, and, unfortunately, my classes were late in the afternoon, precisely when the series games were on.

On one particular day, my fellow Hebrew school classmates and I all brought in small, pocket-sized six-transistor radios, complete with little earpieces. We told our elderly rabbi, Harry Hirschberg, we all had come down with a sudden case of being "hard of hearing" and that's why we had the headphones. We all seemed to be "hard of hearing" on the exact same day, and Mr. Hirschberg, being an honest, sincere man, never gave a thought to the possibility that we could be lying. So the whole class sat listening intently to the words of sportscaster Mel Allen, instead of those of Rabbi Harry Hirschberg.

I suppose that collective lie on our parts was the start of my not taking to religion in any serious fashion. At the wedding of one of my nieces one year, I was asked to say the blessing over the cutting of the challah bread, a marvelous tradition and a great honor. I got up to say the holy words, microphone in hand in front of 200 people, and I thought I knew the prayer by heart. Unfortunately, about midway through it, I got a bit hung up at one particularly tricky spot, and I lapsed into a blessing for *Hanukah*, not *challah*. The blessings were somewhat similar, with many of the same words, but it was one of my most embarrassing moments... ever. I suppose, for me, being a Jew has always been less deity, more deli.

I went to Yankee Stadium many times when I was a kid, but I never did catch a ball. One time, when I was about ten, I was watching a game from the upper deck with one of my sisters. The seats there usually cost $1.50, but this particular night was G.O. night, when, through the school's "general organization," students got in for fifty cents. That was a night I will never forget because Phil Linz, another singles hitter (translation—*lousy* hitter), hit twelve foul balls to our section in one at bat. It was insane. It seemed as if everyone in my area was going to get a ball, and I felt as if I was destined to finally catch one, but no... It was not to be.

Years later, when I had a souvenir stand, it was a few days before a playoff series started, and I was at the ballpark to load up on stock. While I was there, the visiting Cleveland Indians were taking batting practice in front of an empty ballpark. Prior to the start of a playoff series, each team gets a few hours to practice on the field during one of the off days. With only a handful of security personnel, a few cops, and some maintenance and souvenir staff in the building, the ballpark is eerily quiet, with only the crack of a bat and some ballplayer chatter echoing throughout. On this particular night, once I had received my stock, I scoured the outfield stands and was able to abscond with eight baseballs from batting practice home runs, sharing some with a few elderly bathroom matrons. But I didn't really *catch* those balls. I *scavenged* them.

One particular day in 1967, I was hanging out in the right field stands during batting practice, dreaming of finally catching a baseball. I was huddled there with a bunch of other hopefuls, all equipped with our gloves from home, when a ball started rolling toward me. In the old ballpark, before the '70s renovation, the fence in right field was very low, about waist high, so one could lean over, which is what I did. Almost tumbling onto the field, I managed to get my glove on a ball. My heart was racing because, even though I didn't catch it, I at least "had" it, but that was as close as I got. Bill Monbouquette, a journeyman relief pitcher, came over and ever so gently swatted the ball out of my glove, picked it up, and ran into the infield. As I watched him scurry on his way like a deer heading into the woods, I grumbled to myself, "Aw man, I am NEVER going to get a ball."

Monbouquette wasn't the only journeyman pitcher on the Yankees who broke my heart. (By the way, translation for journeyman: *lousy*.) Not only did I show up at the stadium with my glove, I also used to go early... and stay late... for autographs. Now that I am an adult, I cannot understand the fascination with autographs. I guess it's simply proof of being in the presence of someone famous, a written document of sorts, and I was unquestionably an autograph hound when I was a kid.

At the old ballpark, the Yankees would park their cars in a lot across the street from the press gate, and kids would line up along a barricade to try to coax their heroes into signing an autograph. With the new, some would say "elitist" stadium, the players come through a security gate and actually park underneath the field, thus separating themselves from the fans and making getting close to the players that much more difficult, if not impossible. Now, the fans who wait are crunched in tight and essentially wave at the tinted windows of luxurious SUVs. Back at the old ballpark, fans could track a car and follow alongside it as it came to stop signs or red lights and still be able to continue to beckon the player for a signature.

I used to watch for the Yankees when they would leave after a game, and, one time in 1966, when I was eleven, I ran after Hal Reniff, another journeyman/lousy pitcher on the staff. *Wow*, I thought. *I'm gonna get Hal Reniff's autograph — cool.*

So I came up to his car on the driver's side, which was now stopped at a traffic light, and I poked my little pad and Bic ballpoint pen in there and asked, "Uh, Mr. Reniff, can I please have your autograph?"

And what did Reniff, winner of a grand total of twenty-one games in a career of seven Major League seasons, do? He rolled up his electric window, *zzzzip*, right on my outstretched arm. I got it out in time, pad and pen, too, but that wasn't nice, was it? I mean, c'mon! I was only eleven.

Years later, I was working on a film, and I heard a story from Patrick O'Neal, who later owned O'Neal's Balloon, a hip saloon in New York. He had tried to get an autograph from a star actor who had been shooting a movie near O'Neal's hometown in Florida. The actor was brilliant, one of the finest of all time, but he was also known to be a hardcore alcoholic with little patience for his public. O'Neal, an eager young teen of fifteen at the time, had no way of knowing this. One day, he anxiously went up to him and asked, "Sir, I am the biggest fan of yours. May I have an autograph?"

The celebrity glanced at him and simply replied, "Go fuck yourself, kid."

In retrospect, Reniff wasn't such a bad guy.

In the sixties, I would go to Shea Stadium to watch the Mets and try to get autographs there, as well. One Old-Timers' day, I was scrunched in near the dugout as Joe DiMaggio was signing for the fans. Everyone was pushing and shoving, crammed in to get to "the great DiMaggio," as Hemingway referred to him in *The Old Man And The Sea*.

At one point, he looked up and said, "Boy, you kids are going through a lot just for this."

And I quickly piped up, "Yeah, but it's worth it, Joe."

He immediately stopped signing and sternly said, "*Who* said that?"

Oh boy, I was *so* nervous. Joe DiMaggio was scolding me for calling him by his first name. I took a breath and tentatively raised my little arm and, like a character out of Dickens, said, "Uh... I did, *sir*."

With that, he glared at me and then a smile slowly crossed his face as he responded, "Well... you deserve an autograph, son."

Man, I was beaming as he signed for me. I headed back to my seat, clutching his autograph while skipping through the stands, screaming, "I got Joe D's autograph. I got Joe D's autograph."

But April 17, 1968 is one day at Shea that I will never forget. All one had to do was see Willie Mays play to know he was a special talent, the best of his day. He not only could hit for average, he could also hit with power, he could run, he could field, and he could throw. Those are the five essentials of a complete player, and, in Willie's case, he did it with such enthusiasm and love for the game, it was quite simply a joy to watch him. Everything he did was exciting.

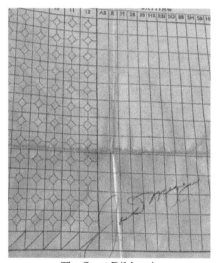

The Great DiMaggio

In describing the very first home run Willie hit in 1951 his manager, Leo Durocher, said, "I never saw a fucking ball leave a fucking park so fucking fast in my fucking life." Willie Mays was my boyhood idol, no fucking doubt about it.

This brisk April day back in 1968, I took the 7 train out to Queens from the Bronx with my two pals, Billy and Arnold. We hung out to get autographs after the game and, to be honest, I don't even remember who won. What I definitely do remember is seeing Willie coming out of the press gate, a pack of kids trailing him as he headed to his pink Lincoln Continental, signing autographs all along the way.

I immediately took off after him but the crowd of people around the car was thick. Willie got in the passenger's side, his driver started the engine, and the people began to peel off. But I was twelve, hadn't a worry in the world, and didn't know or even care where Billy and Arnold were, so I clung to that Continental like a terrier to a mailman.

Luckily, the traffic leaving the parking lot prevented Willie from exiting quickly. I waited patiently, and he continued to sign at his window for the group of us that had followed alongside his car. For me, that signature was gold. Upon coming back to Earth, I suddenly realized, "I gotta tell the guys," so I scrambled across the parking lot back near the press box 'til I breathlessly reached Billy and Arnold, who were waiting there to get other players' autographs.

"Whoah... guys...! You won't believe it... Whooo... Look at this... WILLIE MAYS... whooo... He signed... whooo... my yearbook... *Whooo!*"

Boom!! Those guys were off, flying to the edge of the parking lot, hunting down Willie's car. By the time they came back a few minutes later, after successfully meeting up with him, I was sitting at a curb, staring at my treasure, transfixed by my hero's beautiful penmanship.

Mays still had an effect on me right into adulthood. When Reggie Jackson was retired and had a plaque dedicated to him in Monument Park in 2002, he was celebrated with "a day" at the stadium. For the occasion, he asked for and received Willie Mays as one of his personal guests for the event.

I had a souvenir stand in the upper deck that day and wasn't aware Willie was going to be attending. I had never seen him at the stadium because, to my knowledge, his only appearances were the 1951 World Series (four years before I was born), the 1960 All-Star game (when I was five), and the 1962 World Series (when I was only seven)—all before I had ever set foot inside

Yankee Stadium.

But on Reggie's day, when I heard Willie's name over the loudspeaker, I ran straight out to the stands to see the great one once again. I had left my souvenirs completely unattended, thousands of dollars' worth of stock vulnerable to theft. Just the mention of his name on the loudspeaker had me reacting like a kid again, though, the same way Billy and Arnold reacted back in 1968—*Vrooooom!*

I have to admit, I was a little crazed for autographs back then and my fascination spread to professional basketball players, as well. I once waited for the Knicks outside Madison Square Garden and watched them get into a bus to take them to Boston for their next game. I was fourteen and so excited about getting autographs that I didn't care who signed for me, even if it was the ball boy. The Knicks were usually cordial and cooperative to their fans, and I jumped up to pass my program through an open window to get the signature of one of their reserves, Bill Hosket.

No one would ever confuse the cumbersome, 6 foot 7 Bill Hosket with an All-Star since, in his two years with the team, he averaged less than three points a game, usually getting his minutes during "garbage time." Frankly, he may have been just as excited *giving* the autograph as I was *getting* it. But, just my luck, while he was signing for me, the bus started to pull out, and he froze, not really knowing what to do with the program I had passed to him.

I started yelling at the bus as it was moving towards Seventh Avenue, "Toss it, Bill. Just toss it." He tossed it but, as he did and as I was running along to keep up with the bus, I fell right on my face, scraping my forehead as well as my knees. As the program landed on me, I glanced up at him through his window. A dramatic, guilty look appeared on his face, as if he had caused my fall.

Two weeks later, I went to a game, snuck downstairs during warm-ups, and managed to get over to him and say, "Hey, Bill! Remember me from when you guys were going to Boston?"

He hesitated for a moment, took a quick look at me, and said, "Yeah. Hey, how are you feeling?"

I was only fourteen at the time, and for a professional ballplayer to not only remember me but to ask me how I was, well, that was one "Oh Gosh" moment that has stuck.

One Knick story I have is not a very smart one for me and one I have a lot of regret over. The 1969-70 Knicks were a magical squad: Frazier, DeBusschere, Bradley, Willis, Barnett, and all the rest. They epitomized the concept of team play, and there was no more of a devoted fan than me.

In those days, my dream of being a statistician by amusing myself playing dice baseball and Strat-O-Matic made me very happy to be alone as a teenager. And nothing made me happier than keeping the stats for my favorite team. Whenever a Knicks game would be televised throughout the season, which was about once a week, I kept score in my book. Now, of course, with dish networks and the Internet, a fan can see every game of every team in the league on their phone. This accessibility was not available when I was having my love affair with the team, so, for the games I couldn't see, I would cut out the box score the next day from the newspaper and tape it into my record book.

By season's end I had every game's box score except one, so I went to the library, found it on microfilm, and xeroxed it to complete my season long collection. Needless to say, I was a *HUGE* Knicks fan.

To get tickets for the playoffs, one had to go to Madison Square Garden and get on line at two or three o'clock in the morning, to be sure of getting up to the box office when it opened at nine. It could get nasty, as oftentimes people bullied their way towards the front of the line, since security was non-existent. One needed to stand one's ground, not unlike the days of "drips" at the stadium, when I had to firmly plant my feet to fend off my fellow vendors. Making sure to stash my books away in the closet so my parents wouldn't know I was going to play hooky that day, I snuck out of the Bronx in the middle of the night and took the subway downtown with a friend, waiting for hours in the cold to get playoff tickets.

On May 8, 1970, the Knicks won the world championship over the Los Angeles Lakers in the famous game 7, where an injured Willis Reed hobbled onto the court, hit his first two shots, and Walt Frazier and the team went on to win in a courageous, improbable finish. I had a ticket for that game, but my friend and I, at fourteen, were tempted to scalp our tickets, since the going price out on the street outside the Garden was so high.

I still have this program... somewhere. Bill Hosket is number 20

After having waited on line in the freezing cold weeks earlier, we gave in to temptation. With my extra money, I went on a shopping spree, walking up to Herman's sporting goods store on 42nd Street and bought a Knick team sweatshirt and a basketball. Then, my buddy and I went to dinner at Tad's Steaks, which was a poor-man's steakhouse. For $3.99, we each had a T-bone, baked potato, salad, and a large strip of garlic bread. Then we took the subway back home to the Bronx to watch the game, since the League's rules provided for a blackout on live television, which delayed the broadcast until one minute past midnight. Again, with present-day technology, the game could be picked up on a cell phone, but that's not how it worked back in 1970.

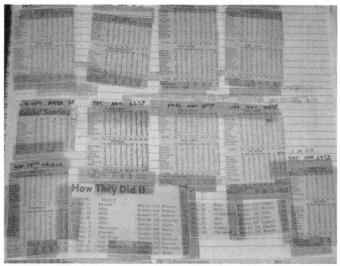

My Knicks record book-neatness doesn't count

And oh yeah, how much did I sell my ticket for to what was later voted by New Yorkers as the most exciting event in the history of Madison Square Garden? *Twenty-nine-dollars.* Oh, the memory of it is like a dark nightmare in my mind. It is one thing I have never forgiven myself for... and probably never will.

In those years, when I was an autograph hound, I would find out which hotel the visiting teams were staying at and hang out in the lobby, trying to corral the players into signing for me. One of my cohorts in my adventures was none other than my mother, Mimi. She was a basketball fan as well, who often told me about when she and two of her female friends beat all the guys in half court one Saturday afternoon at St. James Park in the Bronx, back in the thirties. Since she worked in Manhattan, we would meet up to get autographs before heading over to the Garden.

My mother was what is known as a "kibitzer," someone who is not afraid to talk to strangers. A person could ask, "Where does the bus stop?" and she would take ten minutes or ten years to tell them.

And she was a generous soul in many ways. If she had five dollars, she'd find a way to give you six. She ran to Broadway shows and movies whenever she had the chance, yet she always seemed to juggle three part-time jobs at once. I remember her as a bookkeeper, a receptionist at an eye doctor's office, filling in the shelves at a greeting card shop in Grand Central Station, and various other full and part time jobs.

After a tough workweek, she would finish her supper, do the dishes, and then gather all the newspapers in the house, my dad's *New York Posts,* and catch up by reading the past three or four days' papers at the dinner table. And as much as anything else about her, she taught me to always treat people equally, no matter who they were, where they were from, or what they looked like. Didn't matter. Everyone. Equal. Always.

My mom was a true character: part Edith Bunker and part philosopher. People said she reminded them of the wonderful comedienne Judy Holliday from the film *Born Yesterday*: pretty but ditsy. Pretty ditsy.

She was a hoarder par excellence, primarily because she could not walk away from a bargain, whether she needed the item that was on sale or not. She would often buy something for someone's birthday because she got a good deal, even though the birthday might not have been for seven months or more. The family used to kid her because we had a linen closet that had nine queen-sized sheets. We would say to her, "Mom, we don't even have a queen-sized *bed*."

She also managed to say some things that strangled the English language, like referring to people who give massages as "massage-onists." When I had a cold, she told me to "drink plenty of juices... like ginger ale." And yet, she could also say things that have guided me and made me smile my whole life. Things like:

"People who are cheap have short arms and long pockets."
"If you make your bed, it'll look like you cleaned your room."
"You're gonna buy white pants? They'll live in the cleaners."
"He's too light for heavy work and too heavy for light work."
"If you get bored, go in your room and rearrange the furniture. You'll feel like you're in a new apartment."

Probably her line that I quote the most is:

"Listen to what people have to say, then do what you want anyway."

Is that not perfect? Take advice, let it soak in, and then trust your gut with that extra knowledge under your belt. She also used to tell me, "If you get invited somewhere... go. You can always go home."

Great advice. Both quotes seem to imply "assess the situation and *then* make your decision."

I've actually come up with a few of my own, thanks to her inspiration. Whenever I walk through my door at the end of a long day, I say, "It's good to go out and it's good to come home." Another: "If you're having a bad day, go to bed early."

She also used to tell me, "Rich or poor, it's good to have money," which helped drive me when my vending sales were a little slow.

I've always felt blessed to be raised by someone with such a sensible view. Since she passed away in 1984, I miss her keen insight and pure enthusiasm for life. She is still very much a part of me, which makes me extremely proud.

No doubt her love for theater nudged me into show business. My dad loved his Borscht-Belt comics on *The Ed*

Sullivan Show, but Mom loved the pageantry and glamour of Broadway and Hollywood.

She had her favorites: Dale Robertson, a "Marlboro man" kind of guy with a full head of frosted hair; Telly Savalas, otherwise known as "Kojak," with no hair at all; Lou Rawls, with the golden voice; and Peter Falk, the great character actor.

One day, she embarrassed the heck out of my sisters and me when we waited at the stage door of a Broadway show and she almost knocked Falk down to the ground when she gave him a hug. I only wish she'd lived long enough to see me acting in a couple of *Columbo* episodes. I'm sure she would have jumped on a plane to come out to the studio in LA to say hello to Falk, a big Knick fan as well, who I know would have been as gracious to her, as he was to everyone on the set. And he, I'm sure, would have loved her, too.

When I was a young teen trying to get autographs from pro ball players, she was a great asset. I was awestruck by these giant athletes, but being the "kibitzer" she was, she would casually chat them up, and I would simply hang on to their every word. One late afternoon, we were in a hotel lobby, and one of the Knicks at the time, Dick Van Arsdale, was there with his brother, Tom, who played for the Detroit Pistons. Dick and Tom were identical twins; both six foot five, blond, and good-looking. My mom struck up a conversation with the two of them. They were both very cordial, politely signing for me, and obliging my mother with some small talk.

In the late sixties, the NBA was not as popular as it is today so, in order for the Knicks to draw a good crowd, they would play what was known as "All NBA Doubleheaders," two games for the price of one. These were on Tuesdays, and the first game started at around 5:30 in the late afternoon, between two visiting teams, such as the Pistons versus the Chicago Bulls. The Knick game would start at around 8:35, and this way, by having two games, the Garden would entice the fans to come see a full evening of action. After autograph hunting and then grabbing a quick bite at Tad's Steaks (a tradition, I guess), my mom and I would go over to the arena and catch the second half of the first game and then stay and watch the Knicks.

One thing my mother was never afraid of was sneaking down to better seats. She was often known to "second act" Broadway shows, getting to the theater at nine o'clock and scurrying in with the crowd after they had taken their intermission. Casually strolling into the theater and then heading up to the balcony, she was pretty sure to find an empty seat up there. Post-Depression-era-style, like my dad, I suppose.

My mother taught her son well, since I also used to sneak into seats at various venues in New York. One night, I went with a friend to hear some blues in Carnegie Hall on a night that featured Willie Dixon, Muddy Waters, and Howlin' Wolf. We did have tickets, but they were way up in the balcony, which, in Carnegie Hall, is the fifth level. The auditorium is cavernous and from up there, it's like watching from a helicopter, so my friend and I chose to slink down to a better view.

Security is always very tight at Carnegie. We managed to find our way downstairs and simply started opening doors, hoping to get into one of the lower level circles, as they call them. After some futile attempts, we eventually ended up in a side box on the second tier, overlooking the orchestra section on the left side of the hall.

It was a fantastic concert featuring these blues greats with their All-Star bands and ending in a raucous finale. Once the show was over, the fans were still pumped and cheering for more music but these old-timers did only one encore and were gone.

My friend and I used to bring our harmonicas with us wherever we went, especially when we were to hear music, and this night was no exception. So, as the crowd filtered out, we chose to serenade them with our rendition of "Kansas City," with me singing and him backing me up on the harp. We were rocking the house as the last stragglers looked up at our box, clapping and singing along. As the security guards tried to clear the hall, they were glaring at us, but we kept on playing. *"They got some crazy little women there and I'm gonna...get me one."* I've always told people I sang in Carnegie Hall, leaving out the part that I was being chased by security at the time.

Anyway, on one particular night in 1967, when I was only twelve, I was with my mom and we went to the old Madison Square Garden at 49th Street and Eighth Avenue. While watching the second half of game one, we eyeballed some empty seats down low, so we could possibly watch the second game from up close. During the first quarter of the Knick game, we were busy navigating and, all of a sudden, found ourselves *right behind* the Knick bench.

My mom and I were a good team, because, as I watched the game, taking it in from the lower level for as long as I could, she scoured the area, looking for some available seats. Just then, I noticed that coach Red Holzman was putting Cazzie Russell into the game, substituting for Dick Van Arsdale. We were standing *right behind* the coach, and when Van Arsdale came out, he sat down directly in front of us.

Security at the Garden, just like when I waited for playoff tickets at 3 a.m. in 1970, was non-existent.

"Mom, look," I said. "There's...."

She turned, immediately recognized him, and then did the unthinkable. She *slapped* Dick Van Arsdale right on his sweaty back, almost knocking the wind out of him, and said, "Hey Dick, remember us? This is my son. We saw you at..."

Just then, Van Arsdale turned around. He was white as a ghost, not having the faintest idea who hit him or who she was. Personally, I thought he was going to hit *her*, if I didn't get to her first, but after that whack on his back, I didn't think he had enough strength, so I tugged at her arm and whisked her away.

As we scurried to find seats, any seats, I saw Holzman's horrified look as well, shocked that someone could get so close to even *touch* one of his players, let alone *smack* him. And, being twelve at the time, I realized that, after my mom's whack on Van Arsdale's back, any dreams I had of trying out and making the

Knicks squad were completely shattered.

No chance. No way. Holzman probably wouldn't even let me into the gym.

THE FANS

IT'S OFTEN BEEN SAID, "Kids say the darnedest things."

Wrong! Fans, specifically *Yankee* fans, say the darnedest things. For instance, as the prices went up over the years, I heard a variety of colorful comments.

When the cost of beer grew to $9.50, they said,

"Hey buddy, I didn't ask for the whole case."

"What did I do, break a window?"

"For that price, you should take your shirt off."

"Do I get a lap dance with that?"

I recall, when I told a middle-aged woman with a strong Brooklyn accent how much a beer was, she turned to her husband in shock and said, "Dat's more den we paid in Italy."

The outrage at the price of a beer at the ballpark reminds me of a line from the great George Burns years ago, when he was on *The Tonight Show*. He had gone into a cigar shop and, when he was told his favorite cigar was now going to cost the unheard of amount of $10, said, "For that price, I want to sleep with it first."

Since vendors are dressed in a very specific uniform, which has varied through the years, I was always amazed when people who were looking for their section came up to me and asked, "Hey... do you work here?"

"No," I told them. "I only dress funny."

It also surprised me how, during a rain delay, when it may have been pouring for over an hour, people thought I was privy to the status of the game. "Hey buddy," they would say. "Are they gonna play?" They usually whispered this to me, speaking from the side of their mouth, using a "this is just between us" voice, which assured me they wouldn't tell anyone else, if I gave them the scoop. But, if I knew the answer to, "Are they gonna play?" I'd spend a lot more time at the track than I usually do.

On a typical day, I truly enjoyed being with the fans. They gave off a great energy, and it was fun to interact with them more often than not. But why, when I was selling scorecards as the fans walked in and the temperature was a biting thirty degrees during an April or September chill, me rubbing my hands together for warmth and moving from side to side so I didn't freeze—*why* did people think it was funny to ask, "Is it cold enough for you?"

Oddball queries were prevalent. One fan sought the whereabouts of section 17, and when I told him it was on the other side of the stadium, he asked, "Do I have to walk there?"

Here's another silly question: "How far is the bathroom?" I had a complete set of answers for that one:

"About one thirty-second of a mile."

"How bad do you have to go?"

"Uh, does it matter?"

"Not far... if you start now."

I may sound like a sarcastic smartass, but when people ask absurd questions, I believe they deserve absurd answers. What is one supposed to say to a gung-ho fan in the hallway, full of spunk, vim, and vigor, wearing all the gear—the official hat, the pin-striped uniform pants with matching button-downed jersey top, just open enough to see the official Yankee T-shirt underneath, the head phones so they can listen to the game *while* they are attending it—the whole nine yards. What is there to say to this fan who asks, "Does this ramp go up?"

Think about that one for a moment. "Does this ramp go up?"

I hesitated for a second but ultimately gave him the correct answer: "From here it does."

One middle-aged lady walked around picking up used

souvenir soda cups simply because the word *Yankees* was printed on them. She could be seen scurrying around the lower level with her head down, searching under seats for these sixteen- or twenty-four-ounce plastic treasures. I was not even sure if she'd ever watched any of the game or was even a Yankee fan, but this lady was focused, I'll give her that.

The stadium has always been a haven for lonely souls at times, a place where they could come and forget their troubles and be with like-minded fanatics. One lady in her sixties always showed up with three Raggedy-Ann Yankee dolls, which stayed with her at all times. I never asked, but they may have been from her childhood since they looked a bit worn. She just sat and watched the game with her "little friends." I enjoyed seeing people like her who, in their private lives, may have been a bit peculiar but who felt right at home melting into the crowd in the Bronx.

A friend of mine told me of the lady who came over to his souvenir stand to buy a doll. "It was a stuffed bear with a small Yankee hat on its head, twenty dollar variety—standard doll," he told me. "The lady seemed okay—middle-aged, wearing a Yankee cap. Non-descript—nothing unusual. That is…, until she started to *lick* the doll."

That's right—she was *licking* the doll. She hadn't even purchased it yet, not that owning the doll would have made licking it okay. But my friend, a veteran vendor, he *knew*. Even when he caught a glimpse of a nearby popcorn lady, whose eyes apparently were bugging out of her head at what she was watching; *he knew*. He knew this passionate doll-licker needed to get up close with her potential new purchase, so he had to call upon the utmost patience to make this sale. Which, of course, being a seasoned, longtime vendor, he did… Thank you very much.

Many hardcore fans have come out to the ballpark year after year, through good teams and bad, to cheer on their Yankees. One of them was "Uncle Willy," a short, white-haired, white-bearded man dressed in a cape and sorcerer's hat. During the seventies and eighties, he came down to the Bronx from Kingston, in upstate New York, bringing numerous signs that appropriately and succinctly commented on the action on the field. He brought a carnival atmosphere to the games, and the crowds adored him.

Now, there are fewer and fewer of those diehards, either because of the high price of tickets or because the passion has simply vanished. One fan favorite was Fred "Freddy" Schuman, the Bronxite who would walk around the stadium with colorful signs he'd make for each day's game. He would carry an old skillet and a spoon, welcoming anyone and everyone to clang the spoon on the skillet and get the team going. Though he got a little slower prior to his passing in 2010, he still came out to the new ballpark during its inaugural season, and everyone was genuinely glad to see him. Though he himself said with great humility, "I don't know if the players even know I exist," he was a true fan favorite.

Freddy was indeed known by the players, as well as the Yankee organization, which paid tribute to him with a moment of silence prior to the third game of the 2010 American League Championship Series. In addition, Freddy's Yankee jacket was displayed in the lobby, along with his trademark skillet, for the balance of the season, so the fans could give it a clang one last time.

Freddy put out his own little monthly newsletter, which he graciously handed out for free, simply titled *Freddy Sez*. It proudly stated on its cover that it was "published *infrequently*," and it always carried pictures of fans in various states of optimism. Jokes would usually be included—he was always looking for a laugh.

One tale recalled an old couple returning to a state fair year after year. The husband always wanted to take a helicopter ride, but his wife would say, "That helicopter ride is fifty dollars, and fifty dollars is fifty dollars."

One year, the same conversation occurred, and he said, "Sweetheart, I'm eighty years old. If I don't ride that helicopter, I may not get another chance."

Again his wife replied, "That helicopter ride is fifty dollars, and fifty dollars is fifty dollars."

The pilot, standing nearby, overheard them and said, "I'll make you a deal. If you can stay quiet for the whole ride, I won't charge a penny. But if you utter one word, it's fifty dollars." So they took the ride and the pilot did all sorts of daredevil dips and tricks but heard not a word. When they landed, he looked in his rear view mirror to the back and said to the old man, "I can't believe it. I did everything I could to get you to yell out loud, but you didn't. I'm impressed."

The old man replied, "Well, to be honest, I almost said something when Ethel fell out, but y'know, fifty dollars is fifty dollars."

As far as New York fans go, no one has shown a greater sense of team spirit and given more of themselves for the sake of their team than the woman who sat behind home plate at Shea Stadium during the 1986 World Series. On nearly every pitch from the Red Sox in game 6 (Bill Buckner's infamous night, when a slow roller trickled through his legs for a magical Met win), she swung her arms in a circular motion to distract the pitchers, similar to the illegal-procedure gesture performed by a football referee. I suppose it's the equivalent of a crowd at a basketball game shaking large plastic bricks at a foul shooter, but this woman did this throughout the game, on almost *every* pitch. Watch it on ESPN Classic sometime—game 6, for her beloved Mets.

But that's a Met fan—we are talking *Yankees* here. The Bronx fans can easily be categorized as a special breed, so attached to their team that they feel they deserve a ring whenever the Yankees win the World Series. An entitlement surrounds these people, as if their last name were DiMaggio. And their numbers are vast: when I spend time in Los Angeles, I see more Yankee caps worn on the street than Dodger caps. When I watch the news, I see these caps being worn around the world, from the Middle East to Europe to Asia.

Oftentimes, the Yankee fans in a section take on a personality of their own, whether they collectively razz on the ump, the opposing team, or even other fans. Cleveland had (and may still have) Chief Noc-A-Homa in their bleachers to amp up those sad fans through years of mediocrity. But the crowd in the Bronx bleachers was, and still is, like no other.

Over the years they have come to be known as the Bleacher Creatures, and for good reason. There was a core group of about forty or fifty of these fanatics when they first gained prominence, and individually they rarely missed a single game. They have been immortalized in books, and there was even a T-shirt for sale in the Bronx that celebrated this zealous lot. One creature cashed in on his celebrity and was enlisted to promote a print ad for some baldhead wax, a product to shine up one's dome. That the ad used to hang in the men's rooms at the old ballpark just goes to show that an endorsement from a creature is good for business.

Whenever the Yankees take the field for a home game, the creatures cheer for each position player, one at a time, in a roll call. The tradition continued into the new ballpark, as when Derek Jeter got the shout-out in the static, but concise,

>   DER-EK JE-TER (clap-clap...clap-clap-clap)
>   DER-EK JE-TER (clap-clap...clap-clap-clap)

Or:

>   A-ROD (clap-clap)
>   A-ROD (clap-clap)

The creatures go right on through the whole lineup, calling out each player in the field during the opening minutes of the first inning. And the cheer continues until the player being lauded flicks his cap, waves, or acknowledges them somehow.

Since 1996, when the creatures called out from section 39 to first baseman Tino Martinez and he tipped his cap in acknowledgement, it has become a tradition at the ballpark at all home games. There were two times I am aware of when they didn't do the roll call: in 1999, they were silent when they disagreed with the Yankee policy for the sale of postseason tickets; and in 2010, at the first game played after team owner George Steinbrenner's passing.

Though the creatures are a boisterous lot, they have their own rules. Back when the dance-a-long song "The Macarena" was popular, it was played with the fans in the stands up on their feet and moving to the beat. Needless to say, the creatures, traditionalists all the way, would have no part of it.

They also abhor "The Wave." With many tourists in attendance at games, it has become common for the fans to unite and get involved with this section-by-section cheer, but the Bleacher Creatures remain defiant. Even when the whole ballpark participates and every level of the stadium rises and sits in unison like a large wave, the bleacher fans stay seated when it becomes their turn, often causing boos to cascade upon them. They are a principled lot and their refusal to participate implies, "If you people want to wave, go back where you came from, and wave all you want."

Though the sale of beer was forbidden in the bleachers during the final few seasons at the old ballpark, sobriety didn't stop the creatures from being rowdy. I often heard them yelling to other sections,

"BOX-SEATS-SUCK!"

"BOX-SEATS-SUCK!"

One night, the fans in the box seats answered them with, "GET-A-JOB! GET-A-JOB!"

Back in the seventies and eighties, the Yankee/Red Sox rivalry often sparked fights, especially in the upper deck, where there were fewer security guards than in the rest of the ballpark. Actually, the most disruptive and unruly crowds of all were during "Shield Nights," when the game's proceeds went to the families of policemen and firemen who had died in the line of duty. The stands would be full of men and women in uniform, and the beer and fists would fly throughout the game. It is common knowledge that New York City cops and firemen ("Finest" and "Bravest") don't get along very well. "Shield Nights" tended to bring out the worst in them.

The rivalry with the Red Sox remains heated to this day, as each team's fans can be merciless. I recall a game where J.D. Drew was playing for the Sox in right field, and a fan kept heckling him in a thick, fake Boston dialect. "Hey, Drrrew. Pahrk yur cahr." Eventually this turned into an extremely exaggerated, "Hey, Drrrrew. Pahhrrrk yurrrrr cahhrrr!"

The burring was infectious, as many of his friends joined in with the razzing with this embellished, Irish/Scottish "Bahston" brogue. Then the initial culprit followed up with, "Come on, Drew, be a man. Give me the finger."

Ah, the Yankee fan. "A woik of ahhhrrrt."

One time, I was vending souvenirs through the stands, walking around with both Yankee and Red Sox hats. I was in the upper deck when a boisterous fan saw me and started screaming, "A Red Sox hat! A Red Sox hat!" He was almost maniacal in his request, a bit possessed. "Give me a Red Sox hat. I want a *RED SOX HAT!*"

As I handed him one, he literally flung the money to me while the fans in his section had this odd look on their faces, believing this guy was a little "wacko."

Then he took the hat, ripped it up viciously, and tossed it in the air, scattering pieces as he screamed, "*FUCK BOSTON!*"

As the crowd cheered, I said to no one in particular, "I'm glad I was part of that."

As time went on, that sort of thing was frowned upon, to say the least. Eventually, no one was even allowed to wear a T-shirt that read *Boston Sucks*. If a fan was caught wearing one in the ballpark, they were asked to turn it inside out, and if they didn't comply, they were escorted out. But the hearty ingenuity of Yankee fans was, and still is, a thing of beauty. I couldn't help but laugh when I saw fans wearing shirts that got no discretionary reaction from security at all that read, *SAWX SAWK CAWK*.

During the Yankees/Phillies World Series of 2009, I saw the following incident play out that was tough for even *me* to believe. I had had a scorecard/program booth on the main level down the left field line. During a series, programs sell extremely well, as everyone, tourists and locals alike, feels it imperative to bring home at least one program for posterity. For a regular season game, I would sometimes take a scorecard gate and then, once the national anthem played, I'd check out from the gate and proceed to a station to sell my beer. But for the series, I would always maintain my stand throughout the whole game, since scorecard business was so profitable.

On this particular night, the Yanks were getting beat by the Phillies, and by the seventh inning, some fans had imbibed their favorite alcoholic beverage to their personal limits... and beyond.

My booth was situated in an area right near a gathering place for a crew of New York City police, so there were approximately fifty cops standing within twenty feet of me. At one point, two middle-aged male customers came up who were fully decked out in Philadelphia Phillies garb: hat, T-shirt and commemorative World Series souvenir jackets. There was no doubt they had taken the two-hour drive up the Jersey Turnpike to root for their team.

While these burly Phillies boosters, built like squat football coaches, were purchasing their programs, a pair of young Yankee fans tumbled into view. I say tumbled since they were two of the many who had reached their personal drinking limit... perhaps even gone beyond it. They were mid-twenties, frat-boy types who were speaking in that LOUD voice that is common after one has had three or four beers too many.

Soon the LOUDER of these boys spotted my Phillies customers and, planting himself in a firm stance to support a mellifluous-toned but terribly slurred speech, proceeded to blurt out, "Philly SSSucks C**k."

Everyone within earshot, including the fifty cops, heard this declaration. The two Phillies customers ignored it, since they knew they could deck these two frat boys in a second, if the need should arise for that sort of thing. The cops just scoffed at the remark, as they were primarily gathered together to prepare for the end of the game. The upcoming mass exodus of fans required they be dispersed throughout the stadium for a safe exit for all, and the cops were in the midst of planning their strategy.

In fact, the only one who truly reacted to this remark was frat boy #2. He eyed the members of the NYPD, quickly grabbed his buddy by the chest, and whispered, "Cool it, man. Just cool it!"

With the cops and the coaches in his vision, I would have thought frat boy #1 would have listened to his pal. Instead, he just took a deep breath and pronounced even louder, "*Philly SSSucks a LOT of C**k!*"

I had never seen fifty New York City cops crack up simultaneously before... but I did that night.

Fans can be enthusiastic no matter which team they root for. And Yankee *haters* can be as passionate as Yankee fans. One friend of mine, who lives in Los Angeles, can't stand the Yankees. So, one year for his birthday, I gave him a box with a Yankee cap in it as a present. He gave me a look as if I had lost my mind, but this was a two-part gift. In his second package was a box of wooden matches and some lighter fluid. With his friends circled around a barbeque pit in his backyard, he had, in his words, "the best birthday ever!"

I once had an interesting exchange with a fan behind home plate. He was a distinctive regular whom I had recognized from previous games, since he also sat in a wheelchair, with someone assisting him, as he watched the game. On this particular night, I sold him a beer, and, as I was giving it to him, I noticed a swastika tattoo on his forearm. I stared at it.

He stared at me, then back at the swastika, and then said, "Does that offend you?"

I quickly responded, "It offends the whole human race."

He looked a little taken aback, but I made the transaction without another word being said and went on my way. I can't explain it, but two weeks later, he was again in his section, and I noticed the tattoo was gone. Maybe it had been there for many years and he had forgotten about and neglected to deal with it, but I will always remember that encounter.

Over the years, my basic call has been, "HEY...! Beer Here!" Simple and to the point. Some vendors may say "Beer Here!" Even simpler. One of my buddies called out, "Catch a cold one." A longtime vendor used to say, "Hey, the beer here, beer... Cold beer." Another yelled out, "Who wants a beer?" Another said quite simply, "Here it is." Once a vendor has a line, it tends to stick.

In my final few years I began calling out, "Hey, carbohydrates here!" Late in a game, I might go, "Who needs a beer besides me?" If the Yanks were getting beaten badly, I sometimes said, "Forget the score, have one more." If they had just given up a home run, I usually said, "Fuggettaboutit. Have a beer!" Some other calls were, "Adult Beverages Here." "Who needs one?" "Bottle of beer—Bud" "Beer Man." And the ever-popular, supremely succinct, "*Beer!*"

To get my attention, fans called for me in many ways. I have been told, "Give me two beers, Mac." Or Kid. Sir. Fella. Pal. Chief. Mate. Or Buddy. Chum. Boss. Innkeeper. Partner. My man. *MAH MAN!* And as the beer flowed into the later innings, I managed to get called any number of derogatory terms... But let's just leave it at that.

Over time, management became very strict in making sure we didn't sell beer to minors. In the new ballpark, the policy is somewhat excessive (more on that later), but in the last year of the old stadium, I was required to "ID" everyone who appeared to look forty or younger. Of course, that can be a bit of an annoyance to people who are clearly over the drinking age of twenty-one, but when I asked for proof from women, I often had some curious responses.

A lot to read before you walk into the ballpark

Some women in their thirties were flattered when I asked for ID, because *they* thought that *I* thought they looked as if they were under twenty-one. They blushed, they thanked me, they sometimes hugged me, and a few times they kiddingly asked me if I wanted to get married. One night, a woman who'd had a few beers already was so taken with my request for her proof of age that she looked at me straight on and asked, "Do you wanna have sex, honey?" Forget the hug, forget the marriage license; this woman was ready for action.

The New York Yankee fan can be tough not only toward the vendors, the opposition, and the Yankees, when they are not playing well, but also to their fellow fans. Oftentimes, the scoreboard reveals marriage proposal requests. Sometime during the course of the game, one might hear the announcer say between innings, "Okay. For Jenny... from David. Will you marry me?"

But invariably, most of these proposals are met with a long chorus of boos. They chant, "Don't do it," "Forget it," etc. As Rodney Dangerfield used to say as he tugged at his collar, "*Oooh...* Tough crowd." And the crowds at the stadium can be quite tough in their own way.

One night, some businessmen dressed in suits came straight from work and were trying to find their seats after getting to the ballpark around the bottom of the second inning. One of the nearby fans, bothered by their tardiness and the commotion, yelled out to them, "Hey, Men's Warehouse... *Siddown!*"

Another fan called out, "The vote for best-dressed fan is in. You came in third."

One longstanding tradition, common at all stadiums, is booing when a spectator doesn't catch a foul ball hit into the stands. In the old ballpark, those sitting in luxury boxes were equipped by the organization with zookeeper-type nets attached to long poles, to help them corral a ball that had crept up the protective screen behind home plate. But if they fumbled the opportunity, they *really* got an earful.

When a fan catches a home run off the bat of an opposing player and doesn't bow to pressure and throw that dirty rotten ball back on the field, the fans boo this person mercilessly. I, who have never even caught a ball, ever, often yelled out, "Don't do it. Your nephew will love that ball. Your son will be thrilled to get a real official ball. Don't throw it back. What're ya, nuts?"

But they throw it back, as is the custom, just to get that brief, exultant shout out from the crowd once the ball lands gently on the outfield grass and one of the umps or a young ball boy or girl jogs to retrieve it. It's a cheap thrill for the fans as well as the crowd to cheer this effort, even though the Yankees have actually given up a homer.

Occasionally, I may have briefly been in someone's way when I was selling in the stands. Often I was told, "You make a better door than a window." It took me a while to figure that one out, but in time I got to hear it at least twice a season.

But usually the fans are courteous and invariably glad to be in the building. I tried to have a positive attitude, because I was in a place where people were having, or trying to have, a good time. The losing Yankee teams of the eighties kept the place quiet, and a good payday was rare, but since then it became, without a doubt, an exciting place to work.

Yogi Berra, who seemed to have the right words to say about everything, including sparse crowds, put it well when he said, "If people don't want to come out to the ballpark, there's nothing you can do to stop them."

I had some fans over the years come by and say hello to me, but I didn't have too many regular favorites. I made a point to be consistent in my service to all fans, or at least I think I did. I enjoyed dealing with the kids, and for all the years when I sold beer, I really missed them. With beer, it was often just one gruff customer after another, but when I had any other items I could sell to the kids, I tended to enjoy the transactions more.

One final thought: Some tips for fans. Two-dollar bills aren't funny. Neither are crisp *new* bills. Vendors hate them, because they are difficult to separate when making change, so we crumple them up whenever we get the chance. The older the bill, the better the grip.

Susan B. Anthony coins and Canadian coins have very little use to a vendor. Throw them into a piggy bank or give them away, but please don't bring them to the ballpark. I used to hate getting Kennedy half dollars and Liberty dollars, eventually sticking them in my pocket and tossing them in a jar at home. And now and forever, exact change is a beautiful thing.

If you see a vendor coming up the aisle with a case of heavy beer or a bin of steaming hot dogs or a tray of sloppy soda..., if you can, *please get out of the way*. If there is an empty seat, step into that area, and the vendor will quickly slide by. I know it sounds simple, but you'd be surprised how many people don't seem to get it.

On behalf of my fellow vendors, please have your cash ready. Time is money, so having exact change is great, but being swift with whatever you have is even greater. I absolutely hated when I was called over and then waited as the customer flipped through a purse, a wallet, or some deep pocket to find the money to pay for the darn item. *Have the money ready.* Please. You will be happy. I will be happy. And the guy in your section yelling, "Down in front" may be the happiest of all.

MY FELLOW VENDORS

EVERY YEAR, NEW VENDORS pop up at Yankee Stadium—friends and relatives of current employees as well as people who have answered classified ads in the newspaper during the off-season. Usually, these newcomers last a short time and move on. Former Yankee Gene Michael's son sold hot dogs for a year or two, while Alan, a friend of mine, tried selling Sundew orange drinks and didn't get past the third inning of his first game. And yet there have been some, like me, who made the job a major part of their lives.

Many of the veteran vendors and other co-workers I've known often ended each season with the threat, "That's it. This is my last year in this place." But I was always reminded of a saying from one of my favorite porters, Rocky the Rasta, who used to say, "Dey *all* come bock!" Well maybe not *all*, but most.

Even though we vendors may have had stark differences in personality or temperament, there was definitely a sense of kinship when necessary. When a co-worker was having trouble with a fan, such as getting ripped off of some product, vendors invariably backed each other up and came to the rescue. In addition, whenever there was bad news of an illness or a death in someone's family, a card got passed around in the locker room and money was contributed to a fund for the grieving vendor. Idiosyncrasies aside, we always stuck together when it counted, but we were still an ornery bunch and often would hold grudges for years.

After a union meeting one year, somebody got up and insulted me in front of everyone. We had had some kind of disagreement, but, frankly, I couldn't believe it, and, in fact, I didn't say a word to that guy for over ten years. During games, we were like ships passing in the night as we hustled out into the stands, selling our products. Perhaps there may have been an occasional head nod, but for many years there was absolutely no communication at all.

"Meet me at the bat"

Every vendor has his or her personal story to tell. Manny Gluck was a school principal for decades and worked at the ballpark for more than fifty years. From the seventies through the nineties, fans coming in through the main lobby at Gate 4, where "the big bat" was situated outside the stadium, would see a six foot six, dark-haired man behind a scorecard booth. That was Manny. As our union shop steward for many years, he fought hard for us every time our contract came up for renewal with our employers. I remember some advice he gave me for when I would skip a class in school: always have a friend keep notes using carbon paper, so as to easily get a spare copy. In 2005, his obituary made it to *The New York Times* ("Manny Gluck, 65, Dies, Yankee Vendor No.1").

Kenny Spinner worked at Ebbets Field, the Polo Grounds, Madison Square Garden, and Shea Stadium, in addition to Yankee Stadium. He was the quintessential vendor: a chatterbox who seemed to know everyone and everyone seemed to know him. Kenny often cut me off to make a sale, which is a big no-no in the vendor world, but I forgave him more often than not, because he was such a people person. I thought it better to excuse him for taking the money right out from under my nose rather than get into it with him in front of the fans, which is an even *bigger* no-no. Anyone who went to a New York sports event from 1956 to 2005 probably bought something from Kenny, an original throwback from an era now long gone.

Many vendors worked at both Shea and Yankee and were often referred to as "lifers." The Mets may play at Citi Field now but it will always be "Shea" to us. A handful even vended at other local arenas, such as Madison Square Garden, the Nassau Coliseum, and MetLife Stadium, where the Jets and Giants play. A "lifer" can be spotted by the curvature of their spine, after having stooped over boxes, trays, bins, or baskets for so many years.

Back in the seventies, I got an important tip from one of them. He told me, whenever walking up a flight of stairs, "try to put your whole foot on the step, from heel to toe, so that you can best distribute the weight of your body." Simply putting only the toes onto the next step puts an extra strain and pressure on that part of the foot. I often forgot this bit of advice during the commotion of a game, and understandably so. But when I was walking under the el train after work and could hear my homebound 4 train a station away, I went flying down the street, hopped up the stairs (the ones I didn't get paid for were the hardest to climb), and did my best to distribute my weight on every step.

Jake Early, short with thinning white hair, soft spoken yet fiery-Irish to his core, started vending at the stadium in the thirties, just about the time when my dad stopped working there. Jake slowly moved up to number one in the ballpark in the seventies, which put him as the first scorecard man at the gate behind home plate. When Jake retired, Manny moved up on the seniority list and replaced him.

Every night, once the national anthem was played, Jake would roll his stand down the ramps to check out as soon as possible. That way, he could get to his corner stool at the Yankee Tavern on 161st Street, from where he'd watch the game on TV. Jake would settle in, have a beer, and wait for one of his fellow vendors to come by and give him a lift home.

I never met him, but before I started, there was a vendor named Max Belsky, who worked despite having only one arm. He, like Jake and Manny, also finished his career selling scorecards every year from his perch at a scorecard gate, but he, too, began as a vendor in the stands. My dad remembered him and told me that Belsky would carry his item, usually peanuts, with his working arm and then tuck his vending bag or box under his tiny arm stump or place it down on the ground for each sale, so he could make change with his good hand. I wish I'd gotten to see that.

Another old-timer was Nick Gerardi, a lifer who died the ultimate vendor death. Nick, who looked a lot like Harpo Marx, always shuffled his feet as he strolled through the stands, hunched over his beer tray. One night at Shea Stadium, he was on his way down to the locker room to change into his street clothes, had a heart attack on a ramp, and died. I wasn't there, but I heard about it from other lifers when the Yankees came home that week. The death of a vendor at the ballpark—*his* obit could have been, "He died with his apron still on."

When there was a night game in the old stadium, beer vendors were required to stop selling in the seventh inning or at

9:30, whichever came first. Mitch, another lifer, worked at both Yankee and Shea (Citi Field) stadiums. Once, I asked him which team he roots for when the Yanks play the Mets during interleague games, and, unhesitatingly, he said, "I root for 9:30."

Mitch was also an avid pumpkinseed eater. If there were pumpkinseed shells somewhere near the locker room floor, it was a certainty he was working that game. He was a devoted crossword puzzle player and shared old one-liners with me in the stands whenever he saw me.

I used to love hanging out after games years ago with Scotty, a porter, 'til he passed away. Scotty was a short, gentle man around my age who grew up in Harlem. We would often trade stories about our similarities and differences, beyond the obvious of me being white and he black. We had some great conversations after games on the grass by the running track in Macomb's Dam Park, which is now the exact spot where the new Yankee Stadium was built.

Sometimes he would be a little short on cash, and he'd ask to borrow a buck or two to help him get home on the subway, yet he always seemed to have enough money to buy cigarettes. And the cigarettes he always bought were imported, relatively expensive Du Mauriers. I would kid him that he needed to borrow money to get on the subway but still had enough for the expensive smokes, and he'd laugh and say, "I have high standards, I guess." For that, and so much more, I miss Scotty.

Many of the vendors had nicknames. "Speed" was a big, tall, lumbering guy who walked as slow as a turtle. "Noodles" told me he got his name as a kid, when he once went to play touch football in the rain and a friend said that, from the distance, completely drenched, he looked like a wet noodle. The name stuck for over forty years.

"Cookie" told me his aunt had called him that ever since he began eating Oreos at the age of three; his two-pack-a-day habit continued right into the new stadium. "Bagger" used to keep his wad of singles in his pants pocket, not in his apron like the rest of us. This led to the nickname "Moneybags," later evolving into

"Bagger." The "Rabbi" got his nickname because he wore his religious garb underneath his uniform every night. He hated when the Yankees had World Series games on Friday nights or Saturdays, because, of course, he couldn't work those games. I'm not sure how Nelson got dubbed "Moses," but Goldfarb came up with his own nickname, "Cousin Brewski," a playful homage to the New York disc jockey Cousin Brucie, who used to play golden oldies on the radio. "Brewski," who has made numerous appearances on radio shows himself, was a big crowd favorite who printed up Cousin Brewski buttons and handed them out to the fans for years. I wonder what they fetch on EBay nowadays.

"Brewski" was a large personality who breathed New York. He always appeared to be in a good mood, no matter how business was going. As time went on, when he asked for identification from beer drinkers, he had to pull out a large magnifying glass, Sherlock Holmes-style, to read a driver's license or passport. And when he made a sale, he gave back the customer their change along with his traditional remark, "Thanks for catchin' a buzz from the cuz."

"Brewski" liked to sing during the course of his day, and one often heard him crooning the old Cuban song "Guantanamera" to himself during a game. Oddly, the way he sang it, it sort of sounded like:

> "One time I met her…
> Then another time I met her…
> One time I met her…
> And then another time I met her."

Many of the vendors were what one might call eccentric, which may be the ultimate understatement. One was a chronic liar, dubbed Pinocchio, and if he said he sold seven trays of beer at a game the previous night, it meant he probably sold only four or five. Another vendor stopped for a cigarette break in the third inning no matter who was playing and no matter what the score.

Business could be bustling, but he sneaked into a bathroom stall and got in a few puffs no matter. In the new stadium, there is absolutely no smoking allowed anywhere, but that didn't stop him from his habit. Whenever I saw him put his tray down during those third-inning bathroom breaks, I was grateful again for not allowing cigarettes to run my life.

Redmond made the trip up from Baltimore to work, staying with family for a homestand, and liked to call out the players' names and numbers in the seats, just like the late public address announcer, Bob Sheppard, used to do. At the start of a game, fans often heard Redmond attempt to mimic Sheppard's, "Now batting... number two... Derek... Jet-uhhh... Number two."

There tended to be a lot of downtime as we waited for our vending day to begin. I loved hearing trivia questions in the locker room, because a few of my fellow vendors were incredibly astute at some of the most obscure topics as they passed the time. It was not uncommon to have heard something like, "Actors with toupees... *GO!*" Or "Co-stars on TV shows who hated each other in real life... *GO!*" If I said Vivian Vance and William Frawley from *I Love Lucy*, I won. What I won may have only been a high five from a fellow vendor/contestant, but I *won* nonetheless.

Old *Twilight Zone* episodes got a lot of play, and whatever veteran character actor's name was sought, the Internet on a Smartphone was called upon to settle an argument. Another trivia game was "Dead or Alive?" where someone would name an old actor or actress and someone else stated their current breathing status, along with their major acting credits. Later, a game popped up called "Always Old," for actors or actresses who have looked old throughout their entire careers. Walter Brennan? Burgess Meredith? Angela Lansbury? Always old.

Movie titles were often part of conversation, whether or not they were real films or fictitious and coined for one reason or another. I remember one that was a bogus title of a gay porn movie—*Tom's Dick in Harry*. Love that one.

Another little quiz was the singing of the first line from a

Doo-wop song or R-and-B tune, and "the contestant" had to name the group and the year it was recorded. I was always out in the first or second round, but the regulars rarely, if ever, got stumped.

Rich spoke in the locker room about A.V.D., which stands for "A Vendor Dream." More like a *nightmare*, actually. He told of jumping out of bed because he dreamt he was selling ice cream but had no spoons. Another time, he was selling tuna fish sandwiches. Vendors never sold tuna fish sandwiches and probably never will, but Rich was vending tuna sandwiches in his dream.

> *All the fans were tracking me down to return the sandwiches while all the beer guys are on, like, their 37th tray, 'cuz it's opening day, and there was money to be made. And my luck—I'm screwed, 'cuz I've got no mayo for the tuna.*

I myself had an A.V.D. where I was walking around with a few beers that I was having a tough time getting rid of. When I went back to the station to refill my bin, I looked down, and my three beers had turned into three peeled potatoes. Another time, I thought I was selling World Series programs from a cardboard box, but on closer look, they were actually hardcover books— *New York Times* bestsellers. And still another A.V.D. had me working off of a cart full of soda, candy, beer, and hot dogs, but when I got to the section where I was to sell, I found myself at the Guggenheim Museum, displaying large coffee table art books on Picasso and de Kooning. This is called "taking your work home with you," and when it starts creeping into your private life—whoops! Watch out.

Political talk was very popular around the locker room, but it was rarely politically *correct*. One vendor believed the conspiracy theory that the phrase "Hecho en China" would be our country's downfall. And what does "Hecho en China" mean? "Hecho en China" means "Made in China" in Spanish.

It's in labels all over our clothes, household items, even friggin' cat litter. Spanish people are being catered to, and all the work is going overseas. It's a death knoll. I'm tellin' ya, it's bad enough Home Depot has signs in Spanish, but does the Spanish need to be larger than the fuckin' English? Huh?

For more politically incorrect vendor chat, one night the locker room talk got around to lesbians—who they are, how they look, etc. It was a spirited conversation, as some of the guys were saying how beautiful some women are who favor their same sex in X-rated movies. Then one of the guys piped up, "Come on— ya ever seen a real lesbian? They look like Pete Rose in a wig."

There was a lot of daydreaming, as well, especially from lifers who pondered some career changes. One guy thought about opening a disco in the eighties, where there would be magnifying mirrors in the bottoms of the urinals. "Would build confidence for all the guys," was his pitch. I'm not sure why, but that didn't quite pan out for him, and last time I checked, he was still a lifer.

Vendors tend to create their own calls for their particular items. One guy selling ice cream, who I know for a fact was not dyslexic, got a kick out of calling out, "Das Haagen, here." Other nights he yelled, "Jack Cracker."

One of the regular Cracker Jack guys had the surliest call I'd ever heard. Picture someone making a really sour face, always sounding as if he's in a brusque, crabby mood. He called out to one and all, "Cracker Jack" in such a way fans got the feeling he couldn't care less what the hell the public did with their money. Eventually, he began to get his share of fans, too, as they affectionately grunted back at him, "Cracker Jack," with a similar gruff attitude.

A wonderful bonus to working with a diversified crew is that, through the years I have heard hip-hop, ghetto, New Yorican (New York's version of Puerto Rican), slang, and whatever-was-the-latest-way-to-express-oneself-at-the time in the locker room. Working next to a cross section of New York I heard:

"You hear what I'm sayin'?"
"You see what I'm sayin'?"
"You know what I'm sayin'?"
"You get what I'm sayin'?"
"You feel what I'm sayin'?"

Every vendor had at least one good story to tell, marching to the beat of his or her own personal timbale. One told of his struggles growing up in the ghetto. To help make ends meet, he and his grandmother, who raised him, would breed street cats and sell them. "Gotta pay the rent anyway you can." I wasn't familiar with that level of poverty, and it opened my eyes to a broader take on the human condition.

Another vendor told me a story of when he was in prison. He said he was there for six months and swore he was "totally innocent." He explained how he made liquor out of water and sugar packets for inmates, so he could trade for cigarettes. He said most of the commerce in jails takes place in church, where one can kneel down to pass and trade off things behind a pew.

He had fantastic stories, but I always laughed when I saw him selling cotton candy in the seats. Kids would crowd around him, and it was a beautiful sight, it really was. Looked a little like a Pied Piper. Ex-con sellin' cotton candy in the bleachers. Go figure.

Since the Loge was the smallest of the three levels in the old stadium, there was only one commissary, and it was located on the left side of the field or "Loge-left." Sometimes a vendor would be assigned "Loge-right," which meant he or she would pick up product at the commissary on the left side and then was required to sell on the right side, which meant he or she was "taking the walk." Oftentimes, I saw guys go upstairs after call time with a small, foldable luggage cart, which they stored in their lockers. This cart was used to help carry beer from "Loge-left" to "Loge-right" and was an immediate sign that person would be "taking the walk." I never used one of those carts, but I did try to cozy up to some refreshment-stand workers on that level for one of their unused hand trucks. Amazing what one can get for a buck or two.

A rare thing: a quiet locker room

Years ago, when crowds were small, the vendors of a particular item would get together and make a decision to "rotate" for the first few innings. This meant, for instance, if a station had four hot dog vendors, two might go out while the other two would hang back at the station until the first two returned. Instead of four vendors bumping into one another and flooding the area, "rotating" or staggering made the night go more efficiently and orderly. Our bosses didn't necessarily agree with the technique, so sometimes the business plan was cut short if one of "the suits" from the company happened by the station.

Back in the seventies and eighties, we also used to be able to set up in the corridors near refreshment stands so as to ease up on the wear and tear on the legs. When a vendor stands next to a refreshment stand and piggybacks on the stand's business, this is considered "bar action." Some still try to do it now and then, but the company has prohibited it in recent years. A vendor has to again be on the alert that no one from the company notices, or a suspension for any number of games could be the punishment. Back in my earlier days, when there was a sellout crowd, we would simply stand in the corridor, open cans, and literally pour all game.

When I sold beer during football games, a fellow vendor sometimes would be assigned to get a cart, or wagon, with strong, solid wheel casters for the start of that day's daily partnership. We'd load it up with about thirty cases of beer and start opening cans a few minutes before halftime. We would pop as many as ten or fifteen cases to get started, place the cans back in their cartons, and once the crowd filed out of the stands during halftime, we would pour the beer into cups and sell every last one. This was the ultimate "bar action," constantly selling to the line-up of men waiting for their beer (rarely was a woman at a football game in those days) while we didn't have to trudge through the stands to make that day's pay.

Easy sales can be a glorious rush. When fans gathered around during a busy playoff game and money was flying, it was a feeling like no other. Sloshing through rain delays were the kind of days I surely won't miss, but having fans waiting patiently to hand over money and give a "subway" on top of that—and even saying "thank you" for serving them—now *that's* a vendor's dream.

A game takes on a personality of its own, and a Tuesday night crowd in June, for some unknown reason, could be cheap or generous—it was hard to tell until the first inning or two, to gauge them. Invariably, Red Sox and Orioles fans were always good customers, no matter what day it was. Usually Friday night fans were late, presumably stopping for a drink after getting their paychecks.

If a vendor had worked at the stadium for two years, joining the union was required, assuring a day's work when there was an event at the ballpark. Dues automatically were taken from a paycheck, and, by showing up on time on a game day, work was guaranteed according to seniority, no matter the size of that day's crowd. In order to maintain that seniority, one had to work thirty-five percent of the games during the course of the season, including playoffs. Once in the union, your commission was regulated by your seniority, but at least you knew your percentage was assured.

Oftentimes, a vendor would get to the ballpark, sign in, and an hour later the game was called off on account of rain. Since we only got paid on commission, except for a small stipend of a few dollars known as "show-up money," there would be some grumbling on the way home. However, a fellow vendor might offer up, "Well, at least you got the event." The translation of that is, by showing up, credit is given for that day's event, even though the game was cancelled, and it goes towards satisfying seniority requirements. In addition, union vendors were entitled to a bonus at the end of the year, if they worked sixty-five percent of the games; in that case, making the event had value towards getting to that figure, as well.

Since the season runs from the final days of March through September and into October, if the Yanks make the playoffs, games are often scheduled on Memorial Day or the Monday of the July 4th and Labor Day weekends. Often those games are bargain-ticket days and in years gone by, fans would get in free with twenty coupons off the sides of milk cartons. The team promoted these dates with package deals for families, and they drew what I referred to as "cheap crowds." Granted, it's a very stereotypical assessment, but my feeling is, if Dad wasn't cheap, he'd take the family away to the Hamptons or some such place.

Many times, season ticket holders, who often are the very best customers, give away their seats to their friends on these weekends... and presumably head out to the Hamptons, I imagine.

Vendor lingo is common. Hot dogs were often referred to as "puppies." Cotton candy was called "sugar" or "calories on a stick," and soda was known as "sugar water." When a crowd was cheap, we vendors said the fans were "waitin' for the quarters." That referred to the fact that, instead of telling us to keep the change, the customer hung around after paying for their item and were, therefore, "waitin' for the quarters." If an item was $5.75, for instance, that "subway" of a quarter could add up on a busy night of vending. Most important, when it was a cheap crowd, the "subway" at the end of the night was even more valuable to help compensate for a slow night of sales.

One reason why I was able to recognize a cheap customer is I used to be one myself, back in *my* day as a fan, carrying my little paper bag with a peanut butter and jelly sandwich, an apple, and my notebook/scorecard. When a crowd was filing in prior to the start of a game, we vendors were pretty good at sizing up whether they would be "waitin' for the quarters."

After forty years, some general rules were likely to apply— Asian fans may buy out a whole section, but if any of them happened to buy a beer, they would usually sip it for the whole game, which of course is not good for business. In addition, though one might think these are stereotypes, it was often assumed Japanese fans don't tip, European fans also don't tip..., and Met fans barely even *buy*!

One more thought. There was a great jazz pianist years ago named Earl "Fatha" Hines, who used to say, "If you have holes in the bottom of your shoes... shine the tops." One night, I was selling beer in the middle of a grueling ten-day homestand when a fellow vendor routinely called out, "Hey, Budweiser here. Real beer!"

When I heard him make his call, I noticed something and

tapped him on the shoulder. "Dave, I hate to tell you, but you're selling Miller Lite tonight." With this newfound knowledge, he immediately called out, "Light beer from Miller. Less calories here!"

I mention this because Dave, a bit fatigued from one game to the next, hadn't even checked to see which beer he was selling on this particular night. He had been extolling the virtues of Budweiser, which had been his product the previous game, and was able to make the quick shift to pitch what he was currently serving, once he became aware of it.

Never doubt the ability of a good vendor to switch gears on the fly, "shinin' the tops."

SOME NIGHTS ARE DIFFERENT FROM OTHERS

HAVING WORKED MORE than 2500 events at Yankee Stadium, I can say most of the games were usually routine, with the occasional pitcher's duel here and a few back-to-back triples there.

However, some nights were different from others. For instance, I was there when Chris Chambliss hit his pennant-winning home run to the right field bleachers in 1976 against the Kansas City Royals. The field was so swarmed with fans that after the blast, Chambliss had to return to the field from the locker room to complete his turn around the bases and touch home plate in front of an umpire.

I remember the thrill of Yogi's homecoming after having been exiled by George Steinbrenner for more than fourteen years. I saw various no-hitters, over twenty old-timer's games, Tom Seaver's 300th win while pitching for the White Sox in 1985, the Gay Games in 1994 celebrating gay athletes, Charlie Hayes smothering a pop-up to clinch the '96 championship, Tino Martinez's ninth inning home run against Arizona in the 2001 World Series, which elicited such an exuberant response from the crowd, many thought the loge level might literally come down, Aaron Boone's dramatic home run over the Red Sox in 2003, and the Sox's improbable fourth straight win in the playoffs the following year in retaliation, when they came back from a three-games-to-none deficit to send the Yankee fans home in sheer misery.

Another day I won't forget was August 3, 1979, the day after Thurman Munson was killed in a plane crash in Toledo, Ohio. Munson had been a hero of mine, a gritty ballplayer who did whatever he could to avoid the spotlight in New York, often flying home to Ohio to be with his family on his off days. During a moment of silence for the Yankee captain, I watched Lou Piniella break down in tears in left field from my station near section 20 in the lower deck. I actually couldn't finish work that game because I was so shaken over his tragic death. My diary from that mournful time read:

> He was fat. He was not very good looking. He didn't play up to the press. But he tried. Boy did he try. I could still see him stretching from first to third on a single to center and belly-whopping into the bag, invariably safe.
>
> I related to Thurman. I had been a catcher in Little League, I was chunky, I played tough, and I too was pretty ugly. I always took Thurm's side in arguments, and somehow I could feel what he was going through in that Yankee dugout, sensing his fear and dislike for Reggie (Jackson).
>
> I understood Thurman Munson's terribly private ordeal, trying to simply play ball without wanting to be on the cover of a magazine, avoiding the fanfare in a town that breathes glamour and ignores dedication. His death signifies to me how difficult life really is, how hard it is to do what you want, to love and maintain your family and still do your job. The American dream drags onward....

Some nights were memorable for other reasons, such as when I sang "Johnny B. Goode" to a whole section in the upper deck and managed to get them all up on their feet to do a sing-along. That was fun, hearing them do Chuck Berry's hit, but the incident got me suspended for three games. Curious thing was, at around the same time, another vendor had stolen a key to the peanut storage room, and he also was docked three games. I came in to work after my suspension a few days later and someone said I should have been in on the peanut room heist—"At least you would have made a few bucks."

At another game, I witnessed a beer vendor confronted by a fan who was part of a group of Hell's Angels. Sometimes, these Angels can be surprisingly charming, but this one happened to be more of the stereotypical multi-tattooed, gigantic Igor-type. He wasn't happy with the service, got upset, and proceeded to lift this vendor two feet into the air, beer tray and all.

Suddenly, a fellow Angel grunted, "Hey, if you kill him, he can't get us more beer."

That brought Igor to his senses and the frightened vendor was gently placed down... unharmed. Ya think dealing with the public is easy? Fuggettaboutit.

Special nights have also included encounters with celebrities and politicians. There was always a bit of a buzz when someone famous showed up, and though I often "kept it movin'," I've also said hello every once in a while.

Rudy Giuliani, former mayor of New York, came to more games than any other politician. A blatant fan who often wore his Yankee cap at press conferences, in the streets, and at his box alongside of the Yankee dugout, he arrived with a large crew of bodyguards when visiting the stadium. These men watched his every move, but when he entered and left the seats, he would glad-hand everybody he could. Always looking for another vote, I guess.

Michael Bloomberg, another mayor of New York, would show up at playoff and World Series games, but rarely if ever at regular season games. Bloomberg has a very thick "Bahston" dialect, and I think he was always uncomfortable rooting for the Yanks when the Red Sox were in town. One time, as he was coming in, I said to him, "Please clean up the subway. Have you seen the garbage on the tracks at the R and N station at 59th Street? It's disgusting!"

He did not miss a beat, cursorily replying, "I'd love to, but the tracks are the Transit Authority's responsibility, not ours." I discovered some time later that he wasn't lying.

It has been a longtime tradition for presidents to come to the Bronx to throw out the first pitch on opening day or some other big game, as photos of Herbert Hoover, FDR, and others can attest. George W. Bush was there in 2001, following the events of 9/11, and the security was extremely tight. Metal detectors were installed for the evening's game, and a good third of the crowd missed the opening pitch because of the backup at the gates. Since then, walking into Yankee Stadium is similar to getting to an airport gate, as strict searches have become the norm in the twenty-first century.

The first pitch got thrown from here

Paul Simon has been to many games through the years, sitting along the first base line. Once I gave him a free beer and told him, "This isn't because you are a great singer, but because you are a great *actor*." He beamed—he really did. I'm sure he wasn't used to receiving praise, let alone a beer, for his acting. I liked the shock value of that one.

One game, Branford Marsalis was sitting next to the Yankee dugout. The performer who is handling the "Star Spangled Banner" duties, as Marsalis had done on this particular day, often takes a seat down low. I was selling in that section and, being a jazz fan, struck up a conversation with him. I guess I take after my mom when it comes to that sort of thing.

We started chatting for a few moments, and I mentioned to Marsalis an old-time saxophonist whom I often listened to by the name of Gene Ammons, who had been very popular in the fifties.

"Yeah, he could really blow," Marsalis said, and then he introduced me to his pal who was sitting next to him in the box. "Stewart, I want you to meet Larry Fishburne." That was cool... I gotta admit.

Down that same aisle, I once sold a beer to Anthony Mason years after he'd been a tough, hard-playing member of my New York Knicks basketball team. When the Knicks were winning in the mid-nineties with Oakley, Starks, and Ewing, Mason was one of my favorites.

As I was selling the beer to him and saying hello, something suddenly dawned on me. *Ding!* Right there, behind the Yankee dugout, I put down my beer tray and started to unzip my uniform shirt. "Mase," as he was affectionately known, was looking at me as if I was nuts, but my undershirt that day happened to be a replica of his old uniform number 14, emblazoned in Knick orange and blue.

I said to him, "Ya gotta see this," and once he did, his face lit up. He then told his young son sitting next to him to "high five" me. Glad I still had that old shirt.

One meeting with a celebrity contained a bizarre set of circumstances involving my other life as an actor. Oftentimes, an actor who is auditioning is simply a number, one of many who are anxious to get a job. Years ago, I went to an interview for *Death of a Salesman*, which was being produced on Broadway with Dustin Hoffman in the iconic role of Willy Loman.

When I got to the studio to sign up, I could see I was going to be one of hundreds in a "cattle call" to be screened by the powers that be who make the casting decisions. While on line filling out my paperwork, I overheard another actor telling his friend that Hoffman, who was also one of the producers of the show, actually had attended the interviews the previous day. It is rare that anyone other than a lowly assistant is at these "cattle calls," let alone a star like Dustin Hoffman. Of course, there was no guarantee he was going to show up on this particular day, the day when *I* was on line. So I decided to walk my picture and résumé over to the producer's office, thinking this might give me a better opportunity to read for a part, as opposed to waiting with so many others.

That's what I did—I walked over to the Paramount Building at 1501 Broadway, a grand old landmark structure. It was only a few blocks away, and I went up to the producer's office on the sixteenth floor. When I stepped out of the elevator, there standing in the hallway was none other than Dustin Hoffman, who looked as if he was waiting for someone.

Since I was younger and hungrier back then, I quickly leapt at the opportunity and said, "Are you going to the auditions today?"

And he said, "No, I can't make it, but look for Stanley. He'll be there. He's a good guy."

I immediately hustled back to the audition studio and waited on line for Stanley, whom I eventually did get to meet. When I walked into the room I said to him, "Dustin told me to see you." With that, he jotted something down on my résumé, figuring I knew Dustin really well or at least had some connection to him. Of course, I was not about to dissuade him from that thought, even though my relationship with Mr. Hoffman went back a good... oh, I'd say... twelve minutes.

About a week and a half later, I got a call saying the producers would like me to read for the role of Happy, one of Willy Loman's sons in the show. I was to go to the stage door of the Booth Theater, only the second time I was to have an opportunity to audition on a Broadway stage.

When I arrived, I was told to take a seat in the room "behind the third door on the right." I did as instructed, silently waiting a few minutes in a dressing room for my name to be called to then audition for those powers that be. But surprise, surprise: in a few minutes, who should walk into this dressing room but Dustin himself! He was so involved in this production, not only did he sometimes come to the initial interviews, he was also helping actors with their auditions prior to their going in. This was unheard of, absolutely *incredible* to me!

Here I was, a young actor of twenty-eight with only a handful of Off-Off-Broadway credits (many might say *off-ul*), quietly sitting in this dressing room, practicing a scene with Dustin Hoffman. As I sat there with the script in my hand, completely freaking out *inside*, all I could think under my breath was, Homina, homina, homina. I can't friggin' believe this—I am sitting here with...somebody pinch me—no..., not you, Dustin.

After a few minutes, he came to the conclusion that we were actually reading the wrong scene. Usually, the one who is auditioning is the one with the most lines, but in this instance, he was reading the most lines and he already had a part. So he got up and said, "This can't be right—let me find out what the story is." Then... he left the room.

So I sat there, waiting and thinking once again, *That was amazing*, though I was still trying to focus, since I knew I would actually be auditioning in a matter of minutes.

And that's just what happened. In an instant, my name was called, and I was ushered onto the stage with another actor who was reading for the part of my brother, Biff. Before I could think straight, I was standing on a Broadway stage, looking out into a large empty theater, and doing the bedroom scene talking about getting a sporting goods store.

Except the theater wasn't *completely* empty. Seated in the middle of this cavernous space were the casting director Terry Fay, the director Michael Rudman, the lead actor Dustin Hoffman, and the playwright Arthur Miller. If sitting in the dressing room with Dustin wasn't enough to make me nervous, how about this? Here I was, my voice almost cracking on every line, suddenly in the midst of the most nerve-wracking audition of my life with one of the world's greatest actors in attendance and certainly one of the world's greatest playwrights, as well.

I finished the three-minute audition thrilled I hadn't left a little puddle on the stage, but that's where my vending job becomes part of the story.

The following night, I was working a game. I had been on such a high from the previous day, I'd told a few vendors about the circumstances of my *Salesman* audition. Well, around the fifth inning, there was an announcement and on the scoreboard was a notice stating:

THE YANKEES WELCOME
DUSTIN HOFFMAN

It wasn't long before one of my fellow vendors said to me, "Your buddy's here."

And so, from the fifth inning on, I knew I had to go down to his seat and say hello. Just before checkout time in the seventh, I saved one beer in my tray and headed to the box right next to the Yankee dugout, where he was sitting. Fans were looking to buy the beer from me as I came down the aisle, but I covered it with great care, telling them, "Sorry. No, it's sold. Sorry."

When I got to his box I knelt down on a knee and, handing him the beer, said, "Here you go, pal. That's for reading with me yesterday."

He looked at me for a moment and my heart sank, wondering if he even remembered who I was. As he took the beer and thanked me, he said, "Stewart... right?"

Whew! My name never sounded so good. We chatted for a few moments, and I asked him how my audition had gone. He said something like they thought I was too young, or maybe I was too old, I'm not even sure, but I was talking to Dustin

Hoffman, in the front row at Yankee Stadium, and that's what counted.

In our short conversation, he asked me if I would be interested in the role of Bernard, a smaller but extremely important part. I got out of my kneeling position and stood up, pointed to my vending uniform, and said, "Am I interested? Get me outta this joint."

Numerous phone calls ensued in the following weeks but, again, I didn't get the part. Oh well. As a friend of mine later said to me, if I ever get on *The Tonight Show* couch, I've got a good story to tell.

Jack Nicholson has been to the ballpark many times, often by himself, which astonishes me, since he gets recognized and bothered for autographs wherever he goes. Once, in 1994, he was sitting in my section right behind home plate with his girlfriend at the time, Rebecca Broussard.

A year earlier, I had shot a movie with him called *Wolf*. As it turns out, the night before this particular Yankee game, I'd gone to the premiere in Manhattan and had some photos taken with him. When I saw he was in attendance, I put my tray down and gave each of them a beer on me. We started chatting, and he was extremely cordial. He is as big a star as there is, and yet he's just a "regular guy from Jersey." Some fans in his section peered over and thought it odd that Jack was chatting with a beer vendor for so long, but the regulars down there weren't surprised at all. Just Jack being Jack.

When we filmed the movie in Los Angeles, we would talk basketball whenever we had a chance. One day during the film shoot, I walked into the makeup trailer around 7 a.m. and, seeing him sitting in a chair, said, "Good morning."

He looked up and responded with his classic drawl, "...no sssuch thinnnggggg." Just Jack being Jack.

One other night, I was working down the first base line when I saw in my section one of my boyhood fantasies, a starlet who used to appear on television and had been a real heartthrob.

This blonde was every kid's fantasy girl back when I was ten, my generation's equivalent to Marilyn Monroe.

She was sitting with a few people, and when I saw she was there, I went down to offer her a beer. She looked a little worse for wear, to say the least. It had been over twenty years since I'd last seen her dancing and singing in her prime on television, so I shouldn't have been too surprised.

Before I had a chance to speak to her, she blurted out in extremely slurred speech, "Ya got any mmmartinis, honey?"

Another fantasy... bloodshot to hell.

Dave Winfield, the Hall of Fame outfielder for the Yankees in the eighties, left it all on the field — an exciting player to watch. One game, he was sitting in the stands behind the Yankee dugout because he was injured and on the disabled list. He asked me for a beer, which at the time was $3.50.

I gave him the beer, but he never gave me the $3.50. I waited... and I waited some more, but he completely ignored me. Professional ballplayers are used to getting things for free, but this was coming out of *my* pocket, and I don't give away beers to everyone. Maybe Nicholson or Dustin or Paul Simon, but on this particular day, I was waiting on *Dave Winfield*.

I am still waiting for my money. When I used to see him on the field at old-timer's games, I would call to him, "Hey, Dave. You still owe me three-fifty." Still waiting.

Being from the Bronx, I would often bump into people at the stadium from my old neighborhood, fellow classmates from grade school, high school, and college. The Bronx, of course, was a haven for characters. Some of my buddies growing up were nicknamed Schnozz or Bim (short for Bimbo) or Dunce. For some, I didn't find out their real names for years, but they were all great guys to grow up around. One of them, a good friend, was sort of the quiet type. We used to say about him, "He doesn't say much, but when he does..., he doesn't say much."

One game when I had a scorecard booth, a middle-aged, overweight woman came up to me to get a program. She looked a little familiar to me, but I wasn't quite sure who she was.

Then she suddenly shrieked, "Stewart!" and it dawned on me. She was an old girlfriend of mine who, frankly, hadn't aged well. Hadn't aged well *at all*. She looked like someone who would play pinochle with my mother. Gray and hefty. And when we had gone out together years earlier, her body was, if not a ten, a nine and a half for sure. Ooh, that rather matronly image stayed with me that entire season!

I always enjoyed seeing and schmoozing with celebrities at the ballpark, some of whom I worked with on various acting jobs. Jerry Seinfeld (we did a commercial for Microsoft together). Neil Simon. Chris Rock. Adam Sandler. Alec Baldwin. Audra McDonald. Reggie Jackson (he came up to my souvenir stand, and, regretfully, I didn't think to take a ball out of my display case and have him sign it). Steffi Graf. Henry Kissinger. Madonna. Philip Seymour Hoffman. Lorne Michaels. Spike Lee (who I did a movie with). Tom Hanks (the former Oakland vendor, who I also did a movie with) and James Gandolfini (the most humble guy I ever worked with).

I played Tony's accountant on *The Sopranos* in a couple of episodes, and I particularly remember one scene I did with Gandolfini that demonstrates his character as a man.

The action was at the racetrack with someone taking money from him at the ticket window. The actor playing the clerk was an extra who counted the money just prior to the dialogue that started the scene.

Before the first take, the actor asked Gandolfini to hand him the money a certain way, with the bills face-up and placed in a particular place—just so. Frankly, I couldn't believe this extra was telling the star of the show how to do something (one just doesn't do that), but James did as he was told, helping a fellow actor out. There was no questioning the request, no *star* attitude—Gandolfini simply was working along with this other actor, no matter the role. It showed great class.

His character, Tony, was very intimidating, but to those fortunate enough to have worked alongside him, he was a gentle bear of a man, a true credit to his profession.

One game when I was selling beer behind home plate, I saw him in the hallway. When I bumped into actors who I had worked with in the past, I often felt self-conscious about vending, grinding out some blue-collar money by lugging a beer case.

When I saw Gandolfini, I went up to him, reintroduced myself from the show, and then sheepishly semi-apologized for being a vendor as I glanced down at my uniform and apron. "This is my other life," I blurted out, shuffling my feet in an awkward manner.

He shrugged, shook my hand, gave me a big smile, and said, "That's cool."

It was odd, but when he said that, a simple "That's cool," I realized... it *was* cool. In that brief moment, I thought about how many actor friends of his may also have had second jobs back home in Jersey, whether they were cops or plumbers or electricians or whatever. After all, his mother had been a high school lunch lady and his dad was a bricklayer and a janitor, so Gandolfini was quite familiar with blue-collar work. Looking back on that encounter in the stadium hallway, he quietly reminded me we are all very much the same, just trying to move up our own personal ladders.

The camaraderie on *The Sopranos* was very tight, and I remember a day when we shot a scene during a poker game. David Lee Roth was one of the card players, and the regulars on the show were questioning him about where the wildest girls were when he was on the road with his rock band. When he told them it was, of all places, Salt Lake City, land of Mormons, they were shocked and hounded him for the rest of the day for juicy groupie stories.

The conversation on the set often leaned toward women, and one day I heard two of the regulars discussing their extracurricular activities, sharing some basic tips:

"Twenty-five. They gotta be more than twenty-five or fuggettaboutit."

"Yeah... Once they giggle..., I'm outta there..."

I enjoy meeting celebrities and once had the chance to say hello to Count Basie backstage at a club, because someone I was with knew someone who knew someone who knew someone. Another time, I was in California, filling up at a gas station, when I noticed the great John Lee Hooker sitting in the passenger seat of a Cadillac right in front of me.

I walked up alongside the car and told this great American treasure what he meant to me. I mentioned a song of his, which had helped me to "get over" with a few women, and when I started to sing some of the lyrics, he joined in. Together, in a west Los Angeles Mobil station, we sang,

"I wanna hug ya...
"And kiss ya...
"And squeeze ya...
"'Til ma arms fall off."

Still sitting in the car, he was snapping his fingers as I stood and sang right alongside him. Afterward, he took my hand in his, which was like a big old leather catcher's mitt, and gave me a colossal handshake. Sometimes it pays to step up. You never know who might sing a song with you.

One of my favorite encounters was in 2000, when the Yankees played the Mets in what is known as a subway series. Prior to 1957, when the Dodgers were in Brooklyn and the New York baseball Giants were in Manhattan, there were a number of subway series. When the Yankees were in for the American League and either the Giants or Dodgers from the National League, one could take the subway and see every game of the world championship of baseball. The Mets entered the National League in 1962 but had only made it to the series three times—in '69, '73, and '86. But each of those years the Yankees had already been eliminated, so 2000 was a special year.

For the series, I had a souvenir stand, and everything from hats to shirts to programs sold extremely well to the fans of both local clubs. I knew how popular these items were going to be, and the souvenir room, which would deliver my stock, was running short of just about everything. By game two of the series, some items were completely gone—totally sold out. Thinking ahead, I decided to keep a few precious souvenirs hidden in one of my rolling closets, where I kept some of my surplus. I thought, hey, if Bill Clinton comes by, I want to be sure I have something.

At the end of the game on this particularly busy night, I was closing down when I saw a security guard walking toward me with a short man who looked important. When they got closer, I could see this man was Mel Brooks. The guard said Mr. Brooks was having trouble finding a souvenir, any souvenir, and could I help.

The new stadium under construction

"Could I help? Step into my office" I told him, and I pulled back my barricade and sold him a shirt, pennant, and hat while he autographed a program for me. Brooks is an idol of mine, and we talked about the Bronx, childhood home of his wife Anne Bancroft, and about the neighborhood in Brooklyn where he had grown up. I let him go too soon, because he, like John Lee Hooker, is also an American treasure, and I could have chatted him up for hours.

1996 was a special year for the Yankees because, in Joe Torre's inaugural season as manager, they won the championship for the first time in eighteen years. It was a season during which it snowed on the home opener and that included a play by a twelve-year-old kid named Jeffrey Maier, who leaned over the fence in right field to help Derek Jeter win a playoff game that helped get the team to the series. That started a stretch where they were the world champs for four out of the next five years. Since then, it's been difficult to even win *two* in five years, so it was the beginning of a great era of excellence in Yankee history.

Three of the games between the Braves and the Yankees in 1996 took place in the Bronx, and selling hats and T-shirts from behind a barricade was like feeding fish to sharks, as people bought at a frenzied pace. One of my uniform's pants pockets was constantly bulging with twenties, fifties, and hundreds.

During the course of the games, I had to somehow count and organize my money in bundles of thousands to be handed in later that night. I had had a stand during the World Series twenty years earlier, but the money then was not like it was in '96. My pockets were stuffed with loot wrapped in rubber bands, with the sixth and final game's totals coming in at over $23,000 in cash. As much fun as it was to do that kind of hectic business, it was also stressful, getting downstairs to turn it all in safely to the money room.

On the nights when the Yanks were on the verge of clinching on their home field, we would often get championship shirts and hats sent up to our stands around the seventh inning but were given strict orders not to display them until the game was over. Nothing could be more embarrassing for the team than to get championship items out in the marketplace with the possibility that the team might actually lose to a last minute rally. As we know oh-so well, in sports and in life, "it ain't over 'til it's over."

One day before a regular season game, I was wasting time scouring through the maintenance level of the old stadium, where old seats and discarded hot dog wagons went to die.

There I came across a box of World Series tickets that had been prematurely printed up in 1995.

That year was Don Mattingly's closest brush with becoming a champion for the Yankees, a feat he never accomplished during his wonderful career. Playing a best-of-five playoff series against the Seattle Mariners, the Yanks won the first two games at home and thought they were sure to move on to the next playoff round and then to the World Series. Unfortunately for them and their fans, they proceeded to go out to Seattle and lose the next three games, thus quashing their chance to get to the Series. They had been winless in Seattle, and Yogi's line lived on again: "It *ain't* over 'til it's over." The team had prematurely printed World Series tickets in anticipation of them winning in Seattle, but they never did make it to October that season.

For me, the highlight of the '96 series was actually hours after the clinching of the championship in game six. The game ended about 11:30 p.m., but I wasn't finished with my work for a few more hours. By the time I had turned in my money and inventoried my stock, it was 3 in the morning, and all the celebrating was over and the team and fans had all gone home. By that time, the cops in the basement police station were already off-duty and partaking in a keg of beer. My friend Lonny, who had helped me with my souvenir stand that night, joined some of the cops I knew, and we all had a drink celebrating the Yankee win.

While walking through the corridors under the stands a little later, after we were finished with our work, we noticed the left field fence had an opening. Feeling rather celebratory and brazen, we strolled onto the outfield. With my employee badge dangling around my neck, I knew we could at least get away with it for a little while, 'til we got chased. There may be no better sensation for a baseball fan than walking onto the field at Yankee Stadium and looking up at that cavernous sight of grandstands and rows and rows of seats. But the night was young....

Since there was virtually no security at this time and the

only people in the park were a few of the day laborers who cleaned up the stands after each game, we continued out to the bullpen. I hadn't realized what a lousy view a relief pitcher has to watch a game until I was out there myself. Lonny and I sat where relief pitchers John Wetteland and Mariano Rivera waited before coming in to do their magic and then proceeded to head back inside under the stands.

As we passed the pressroom, locker rooms, security rooms, and such, we noticed the ramp that leads into the dugout. Without much hesitation, ready to flash my badge at a moment's notice, we took the same walk that the new world champions had taken only hours earlier.

If I'd thought sitting in the bullpen was a thrill, sitting in the dugout was even more so. There we were in the seats that not only Joe Torre and Don Zimmer had sat in and strategized throughout the whole season, but Gehrig and Ruth spent some time here also, as well as Mantle, Yogi, and Munson. We lingered as long as we could, leaning on the top step, strolling down to the Gatorade tank, the bat rack, helmet rack, etc. Of course, we weren't supposed to be there, and of course we were going to be thrown out, and of course... here comes somebody *right now* in a suit and tie that looks like the "walkie-talkie" type for sure!

We sat and waited for the inevitable as this man strolled towards us from out of the shadows near home plate.

Lonny took the initiative by calling out with a big laugh, "We were just going. Taking in the Yankee win and all, you know," and we rose to our feet to take our leave.

The pudgy, balding man in the one-size-too-small gray suit coming toward us, however, was *not* security after all. He was, we would learn later, George Steinbrenner's ex-chauffeur, and upon closer examination, we could see a drink in his hand.

What a relief it was when he came out of the darkness and remarked, "Some fuckin' game, huh?" So, with the Yankee owner's ex-driver in our company (he told us his ex-boss was actually crying when the game ended), we knew we'd be able to stick around.

While schmoozing with him, we noticed the field was starting to get a little crowded. Some of the off-duty cops had found their way onto the infield and were horsing around. Lonny and I looked at each other with peace of mind, so we took a home-run trot around the bases, which happens to be a lot longer than it looks.

The basement and walkway leading from the Yankee locker room to the dugout

I then sat back in Joe Torre's spot in the dugout and lit up a cigar I had brought to the game for the winning occasion. Just as I started to take a puff, what do you know, the dugout phone rang! Again, I thought the head of security had finally spotted us from high up in the press box, so I hesitantly picked up the phone expecting the worst.

"Hello," my voice cracked, and someone on the other end asked, "Do you want the righty or the lefty?" I played along and called for the lefty, and someone, not sure who, came running in from the bullpen, living out his childhood fantasy for one brief moment.

The visiting team's dugout bathroom — the Red Sox peed here

I've relived this night in my mind many times when any and everyone who should have tossed us out was off partying the Yankee victory somewhere. It was as if the doors to Yankee Stadium were left open and the keys were sitting on the pitcher's mound, a once-in-a-lifetime occurrence on the very night when the team brought home the world championship. After so many years of working as a vendor, my little yellow employee badge proved to be invaluable. On the same field where Wade Boggs had been celebrating by riding on a policeman's horse only hours earlier, I walked and ran where America's heroes once walked and ran, and it felt great.

The view from the dugout

A few weeks later, I found myself up in Cooperstown at the Baseball Hall of Fame, a trip that had had been planned for weeks. While strolling through this fabulous museum, looking at all sorts of souvenirs from the game's great history, I inquired to a security guard about speaking to someone about making a donation.

As anyone who has been to the Hall of Fame knows, there are various kinds of minutiae throughout the museum, from old programs to ticket stubs to even a replica of Lou Gehrig's old locker. The guard escorted me down to the basement, where I saw some other items in storage—old broken bats and such, things that hadn't quite made the grade for one reason or another. I assumed they didn't have enough room upstairs for Carl Yastrzemski's jock strap.

I spoke to someone who was on the board of directors and told him about my Yankee job, asking whether he would be interested in a donation of some of my vending items. He said sure and gave me his card. When I got back to the city, I sent him a package that included an old apron, a pair of crusty, smelly sneakers that had endured the past season, and, lastly, one of my price badges. Two weeks later, I received a phone call.

This board member was very gracious and told me the Hall's response. The apron was a little bit large for display, and he didn't think he could use it, "But thanks anyway." The sneakers were a little too old and crusty, and he didn't think he could use *them*, "But thanks anyway." On both accounts, I told him I wasn't insulted and to simply trash the items. The sneakers were done for the year, and I knew I could get another apron at the start of the next season.

In regards to the price badge, however, he said he could possibly find a spot for that and was very grateful. I was pleased. Somehow, I had found a small place in the great historical shrine of baseball's history, and maybe my badge is on display in one of the exhibits, or maybe it's in the basement with Yastrzemski's jock strap, but it's at the Hall nonetheless.

What's just as exciting to me is, a week after that phone call, I received an envelope with the Baseball Hall of Fame's insignia on it. Inside was a lifetime pass, a symbol of the board's appreciation for my donation. What a month! First, I get the opportunity to run on the field hours after the team wins the championship, and then I receive a pass to visit the Hall for free anytime I want.

When I was about ten, I had snuck into the dugout and grabbed Frank Howard's towel and now, thirty years later, I was just as thrilled, again sneaking into the dugout and pretending to be a ballplayer. Some people get expense accounts or company cars as perks in their jobs, but that stuff doesn't mean much to me. Goofing around on the field, running the bases at Yankee stadium, and having a lifetime pass to the Hall of Fame... **Now that's** *what I'm talkin' about.*

NUMBERS

EVER SINCE I STARTED playing dice baseball in the back seat of our family car, I have been fascinated with numbers. Right into adulthood, I knew that any multiple of 2 for 7 is a .286 average and 3 for 11 is .273. Can't remember what I had for breakfast, as the saying goes, but 9 hits in 24 at bats is .375—*that* I know.

Baseball, of course, is a game of numbers. Most baseball fans know who wore number 2 for the Yankees, as well as number 7 and number 8. The number 24 is synonymous with Willie Mays, and number 44 is forever connected to Hank Aaron.

Numbers also come into play with the game itself, not just on the back of a player's uniform. When a player gets six singles in a game or a pitcher strikes out four players in an inning (both have been done), sportscasters and fans quickly go to the record books and dig up some old player's name who achieved the same feat years earlier. Then the new name becomes immortalized forever with the old name, or at least until someone breaks *their* record.

Some feats, usually associated with a player's endurance during the very early days of baseball, remain in the books for decades. That's why Jack Chesbro is remembered for winning forty-one games in one season for the American League record and Cy Young's 511 lifetime victories have stood the Major

League test of time.

    Many numbers have become iconic over generations, such as 56. Joe DiMaggio's record for hits in consecutive games, set in 1941, comes up whenever another player builds a streak of their own; then the number 56 appears all over the media. 714 is synonymous with Babe Ruth's career home run total, and even though it has since been surpassed, it remains a special number in baseball history. 3,000 is the benchmark for lifetime hits for a batter, as 300 wins is the magical victory total for a pitcher. These numbers are etched in our collective minds, reinforced whenever they are approached from era to era.

    Sometimes, I think of numbers in relation to my vending life. I obviously can't remember exactly how many baseball games I may have worked in any particular year, but I can assume that I worked seventy a season. I know I did that for thirty years at that pace, so that's 2100 games. For many years, I was at every single game, whereas, in my final years, I skipped a few, but tack on another ten years working fifty or more and it's easy to determine I have worked more than 2500 games. That figure doesn't include at least seventy-five playoff games, fourteen football games during my first few seasons, and the occasional visit from a pope or rock band here and there.

    Since I started as early as I did, I was also involved in more World Series than Derek Jeter, Mariano Rivera, or Joe Torre. Except for the handful of vendors with seniority above me, few in the history of the Yankee organization (perhaps Yogi Berra or the longtime announcer Bob Sheppard) were employed for as many playoff or World Series games as I was. And I didn't lose one game; they were all victories for me (*Ka-ching!* $$$).

    Joseph Mankiewicz, Oscar-winning writer, director, and producer, once said, "There's nothing as real as money." When I think of numbers, I always think of the cash that has passed through my fingers.

    I made about a hundred transactions a night and occasionally more, sometimes for one beer, sometimes for two. When I do the math, I've probably taken money from more than

200,000 people. Who can guess where those bills were during their lifetime or in whose dirty hands?

Over the course of each of my last ten seasons, I handled approximately $150,000 a year. For the ten years before that, roughly $100,000 a year, and the years prior, perhaps $50,000 for each of fifteen years or so. That means, in the forty years I worked in Yankee Stadium, I made change for more than three million dollars!

Comparing that figure to some player salaries, Alex Rodriguez's well-publicized long-term contract was for $25 million a year. A baseball player's spring training starts in February, and the season can run through October, if the team makes the World Series—a total of eight months. That means Rodriguez earned over $3 million a month, which was the same amount I handled over forty seasons. And I didn't *make* that three mill—I just *handled* it. I'm just sayin'.

I always loved numbers, and when I was in high school, I was the statistician for our football team for a year. One game was at Randall's Island, just under the Triboro, now Robert F. Kennedy, Bridge.

I was a husky, pimply-faced kid wearing glasses on the sidelines, and one of our running backs came over to me at halftime. He was a top rusher in the city but hadn't had a very good first half—I think he ran for a total of twelve yards. His stats were important for him in order to get a college scholarship at the end of the year, so he trotted over to me for a little "man-to-man."

He was a strong, bulky athlete, and he leaned over my shoulder and aggressively said, "Hey, what about my twenty-five-yard run? Were you cleaning your glasses on that one?"

So I gave him fifty-three yards for the first half instead of the twelve he really had. That's when I knew being a statistician might have its own dicey politics in the big, bad world out there.

There was a famous peanut man in Los Angeles named Roger Owens who sold 6,000 bags of nuts in one three-day weekend. Yes, there was a *famous peanut man* in LA, who had such accurate form, he threw behind his back and between his legs and even appeared on *The Tonight Show* numerous times. According to his biography, he claimed his single-game best was 2,400 bags during a Monday night football game. That figure is astounding to me because, in today's money, a vendor would make $2,000 in commission. *$2000—vending?* Not gonna happen.

In New York, hogging the spotlight with that kind of state fair routine, the other vendors might put some sort of contract out on him. In the Bronx, vendors coerce sales with "daz haagen" and "Cousin Brewski," but if anyone thinks they can get away with throwing bags through their legs and stealing all the customers... fuggettaboutit!

Someone once reminded me that I sold forty-three cases of beer against the Oakland A's in a playoff game one year. "In the uppers on the right side," he said.

I myself cannot recall these specifics, because my motto in the ballpark was, "Same shit... different team." But, on the other hand, I have no reason to doubt "Jughead." He worked at the ballpark even longer than I did.

At today's stadium, a vendor couldn't possibly sell forty-three cases in one game. No way. It's a Jack Chesbro-type number, he of the forty-one-win season. First of all, the beers in the old ballpark were only twelve-ounce cups or cans, whereas today they are bottles that are sixteen ounces, twenty ounces, and, in some instances out of certain stations, twenty-four ounces.

Another hindrance to those big numbers is that vendors can now only sell one beer to a person, due to alcohol awareness. Back when I sold forty-three cases, there was no limit on how many beers a person could buy; the limit was how many they could *carry*. In addition, asking for identification has slowed vendors down. In the old days, that rarely came into play. Unless the customer clearly looked like a minor, I sold a beer to just about anyone, so long as I got paid. The new stadium is asking vendors to ID every customer on every transaction, no matter how old they look, so business is even slower.

Upper Right

I have it on good authority that the record for selling beer in one day goes to Fred Griffiths, with sixty-five trays of "drips" at a Memorial Day doubleheader in the eighties. Apparently, a lot of variables worked in his favor. First of all, it was a doubleheader, so he had two games to sell his item. In addition, many vendors took the day off since holiday crowds are not the best for business. With the refreshment stands short-staffed, Fred had an overrun of customers and a beer-selling frenzy. *Sixty-five trays.* In my last few seasons, I sometimes struggled to sell even three or four for a game.

Whenever I think of Fred, I recall one night in the late

nineties when we went out for a drink after a game. We often went for a beer or two at a bar that was right under the subway, across from where the current stadium is now. We were there pretty late, and one guy came in and seemed to know the bartender very well. What was unusual was this guy asked for a drink to go, and Fred and I couldn't believe it when the bartender poured some ice into a sixteen-ounce to-go cup and filled it to the brim with vodka. Virtually a Big Gulp of Vodka! There was enough in there for a Russian bobsled team.

The subway above that bar where we had that drink reminds me of another number... 4. For as long as I was employed at Yankee Stadium, I took the 4 train to get there. I witnessed the behavior of commuters on that particular subway line, behavior that did not markedly change throughout the forty years I took that train.

Passengers who are Yankee fans have always been abuzz with talk of highlights of the previous day's game: the strength or weaknesses of the team's bullpen, and arguments about trades made and trades not. When I looked up from my newspaper, it was fun to see tourists, as well, either brimming with enthusiasm about heading to the iconic ballpark or filled with dread as they jostled with native New Yorkers, all crunched and crammed in together. Some of these tourists had a look of sheer terror on their faces as, to their left, they shared a handrail with punks with nostril earrings and, to their right, members of ethnic groups they didn't even know existed.

The 4 train cuts straight though the center of the borough, so when I lived with my family at the north end of the Bronx, that was my way of getting to and from the game. The station stops I passed are emblazoned in my memory—Mount Eden Avenue, Burnside, Fordham Road, Kingsbridge Road, my stop Bedford Park Boulevard, with Mosholu Parkway and Woodlawn still to go at the northern end of the line. Once I moved to the city, I would take the train heading south and go to 149th Street and the Grand Concourse, 138th and the Grand Concourse, 125th and Lexington Avenue, and then my stop, 86th Street and Lexington

Avenue. Now that I think about it, that ride home on the 4 train was pretty quick; it was only 4 stops.

Just prior to getting to 161st Street, when the subway car came barreling out of the tunnel from Manhattan, the sight of the old stadium and its magnificence was truly breathtaking. After being in darkness for the ride, seeing that vast shrine staring back, literally glistening in the daylight, was pure joy. Prior to the nineties, the front of the first subway car had a window to peer out from. I did that practically every time I took the train, and the view coming out of the tunnel was spectacular. Didn't matter which team you wanted to win, you wanted to see that view.

It's funny how we think of numbers when recalling the past. In upstate New York, where I worked in resort hotels around the time I started in Yankee Stadium, I once did thirty-nine straight days as a busboy. I remember that number distinctly because, in our living quarters, which housed four waiters to a room, I wrote a calendar on the cheap drywall and clicked off the days to Labor Day, when I would get to go back home to the city. The rooms were in poorly made bungalows, and my work calendar was barely legible alongside the decades of graffiti that graced those walls.

I served lunch to sixty-seven people one day in a hotel dining room in Miami Beach many years ago—all "seatings" were no more than eight to a table, mostly four and "two-tops." During Christmas break from school, I worked for two straight weeks, coming home with about $35. I put in about ten hours a day, serving the hotel's guests, and spent the rest of my pay partying in Miami Beach.

I was on my feet most of the time, but I learned a lot about the concept of volume, which is what vending is all about. It was so hectic that, to save time and valuable space in the kitchen laundry, rather than replace linen tablecloths when customers were finished eating, we would cover one with another. The guests would depart, and we would put a clean cloth right on top of a dirty one so, by the fourth seating, the plates and water glasses had a difficult time staying balanced.

Roger Owens, in telling his story of forty-five years of vending, wrote that he gradually started to feel the stress in his knees. Since I vended for almost as long, I felt that same weariness those last few years, as well. My thighs may still be solid from climbing all of those steps and ramps, but my knees, my back, and sometimes my neck—they've all said "hello" to me at the strangest times.

Getting dressed for a game during the last few years, I allowed myself some extra time to put on my weight belt to protect my spine, my ankle brace, a wrist apparatus because of the beginning effects of arthritis, and leather gloves with the fingers cut off, so as to be able to make change and preserve my hands from calluses. And, oh yes, before I took out my first tray each night, I had to stretch out for a good five to ten minutes, so my legs didn't tighten up. I didn't have to do that when I started as a teenager in the seventies. Seniority has its downside, that's for sure.

One of the factors that affected those aches and pains was the consecutive-day homestands that the team sometimes played. When I was younger, I used to think, "Great. Make all this money in a short period of time and then, when the team is on the road, I'm free to run around a bit." But, as time caught up to me, I sorely needed a day off.

When the schedule came out during the winter off-season, vendors stared at it closely. I imagine the ballplayers did the same, to see how the year would play out. There might be ten straight home games, nine out of ten, or eleven out of twelve. One stretch actually was fifteen straight, as a rain-out game from earlier in the season was re-scheduled on a day set aside for travel for the team. That was tough. I recall lots of dirty laundry drying out in my apartment for those weeks.

In moments of self-doubt, from my teens right into my

thirties, I was a little self-conscious about my job as a vendor (make that a **lot** self-conscious) and I thought to myself, *What will people think? I mean—I've been here ten years.* No one is at a part-time job for ten years—I mean, no one is at a part-time job for eighteen years—I mean, no one is at a job for twenty-six friggin' years.

I think my gut fear was running into an old teacher, any old teacher. I often thought that vending was not a worthwhile job, that it was beneath me. As years went by, I realized the difficulties of life, what hardships *really* are, and my level of acceptance grew. Compared to *truly* hard work, fifteen straight games... or serving lunch to sixty-seven people... really wasn't all that bad. A job is a job.

Making money on a commercial doesn't mean my acting work on that commercial was any better than my acting work doing a play for free. Some days are easier than others, and some paydays are better than others. Time taught me not to worry about bumping into James Gandolfini or even my old second-grade teacher, who might look down her nose at me. When I bumped into a teacher at the stadium in 1970, he'd helped me get the job in the first place.

When I went on acting interviews, people asked me what other job I had, and I often said I was in "sales." It's true. I "sold" things in Yankee Stadium. Sometimes, I would say I was a "food distributor." After all, nobody likes to lie.

Over time, thankfully, my self-consciousness subsided, but often I would see people look at me in a condescending way when I said I sold beer in Yankee Stadium. Then they might say, "If you don't mind my asking, how much do you make for a typical game?"

I heard that question a lot, and whenever fans asked me in the ballpark, I always had a stock response—"How much do *you* make?" That would invariably shut them up real quick.

I don't think it's anyone's business how much anyone makes—it's not my decision to write the check for Alex Rodriguez or for some big name actor in his or her latest film. The funny thing is that on the odd occasion when I would tell people how much I actually did make for a game, after they'd been looking at me with disdain, their response was often, "Can you get me a job there?"

With James Gandolfini on the set of THE SOPRANOS

Numerology was most important when it came to a vendor's seniority. The difference of just one number could prevent a vendor from getting the item he or she wanted or the location, and, over the course of a year, that could amount to an extra ten to fifteen percent in earnings.

Our badge number indicated our seniority and, back in the seventies, there was a dispute as to the exact day when two vendors had joined the union, which never did get settled because of some shoddy paperwork. As it turned out, those two became a shared number—for years they were "8A" and "8B." They somehow worked it out, and when they both ultimately decided to get souvenir stands, they actually split their income. So, if one of them made $300 for a game and the other made $400, they split the difference.

I was always behind them in seniority, ending my career as number 15. I was often glad when Jerry, who was one number ahead of me, didn't show up for work, so I moved up on the list, while Carl, who was one behind me, never seemed happy to see me in the Bronx.

Some final thoughts on numbers. In the game of baseball, if a player fails to get a hit in seven out of ten times at bat, he is considered a superstar. In fact, if he does it long enough in his career, he will most likely get into the Hall of Fame, as a lifetime .300 hitter. No other sport allows you to succeed only three times in ten attempts and considers you excellent, one of the greats of the game.

There is an "ages- of- man" metaphor that pertains to vendors. At twenty, you think, "Cool. I'm working at the stadium, and I get to see the games for free." At thirty, you think, "Jeez, I hope I don't bump into my kindergarten teacher. I could never live it down." But at fifty, you think, "Aaah, who gives a shit!"

CHARACTER DRIVEN

I TELL PEOPLE New York City is a place you either love… or you're dead. To me, having grown up in New York, the rest of the country is just a train set.

When I lived in the Bronx, a trip to Manhattan was always special. "The City," as we called it, was cool. In my early teens, I would go downtown on the subway and hang out at Macy's department store on 34th Street, playing and causing minor havoc in the sporting goods section for a few hours, then goofing around on the escalator for another two hours.

Years later, I would meet people who played chess and backgammon at clubs late at night on 86th Street on the East Side, 72nd Street on the West Side, or in the East Village. At the end of the night, I'd follow it up with an order of Chow Har Kew in Hong Fat's on Mott Street in Chinatown at three in the morning.

Make no mistake: this was not what I was used to up in the Bronx. In my neighborhood, I primarily had Jewish classmates who I played Little League with, hung out with, and did predictable things with (though we did, of course, love Chinese food). Going into The City opened my eyes to a diverse new world, filled with people from far-off lands who said and did unusual things.

In New York, when I go to a local laundromat, there are often women there who provide the service of doing wash for people who drop it off on their way to work. These women, who tend to come from Mexico, Central, or South America, strive to maintain native tradition by eating homemade foods during their lunch breaks. As I folded my laundry, I would see their tamales, wrapped tightly in aluminum foil, kept piping hot in the emptied but warm dryer machines.

I have always said, if you open your eyes, New York will entertain you. Central Park can be very entertaining for people-watching. I'll never forget seeing an elderly woman attempting to walk her dog. The woman was very well dressed, "old money" as they say, probably from Park or Fifth Avenue. The dog may have been a show dog: a little white poodle with pink ribbons in her hair and, I presume, spoiled to the max.

I was about to go into the park for a run around the reservoir when I saw this lady impatiently standing over her pet, sternly arguing with the little "darling." She looked down at the poor thing, which was stubborn and refused to get up from its position. Eventually, she couldn't take it anymore and pleaded to the little pooch, "…What do you take me for…? An idiot?"

Another time in the park, I was with a friend, and we saw a man who had an extremely long beard as well as extremely long hair, both the same length and color. My friend Ken, a quick-witted New Yorker himself, turned to me and said, "You have to pull that guy's pants down to know if he's comin' or goin'."

And on a recent trip to the city, my wife and I overheard a heated conversation on a park bench between a woman and what appeared to be her cute little six-year-old daughter. After a few moments of eavesdropping on their bickering, the last line we heard was the girl telling her mom, in an exasperated tone, "*Aah*, quit complainin'!" Life comes at you real quick in New York.

When there was a game at the old stadium, there were enough policemen in the area to warrant a station being built in the basement of the ballpark. A transit cop at the 4-train platform was a friend of mine who checked in at this ad hoc precinct house. Sometimes, to keep their sanity, he and his partner would quiz scofflaws, who were attempting to avoid paying their fares, to see if they were mopes. According to the web-based *Urban Dictionary*, here is the definition:

> **Mope:** *n. (mohp)* A person of lower socio-economic status that leeches off the greater good of society, is lazy and is normally involved in some sort of criminal activity.

The quiz these partners concocted, however, presented a mope as something to aspire to, something of value, and, in this instance, it actually *was* of value, as the cops would let them off without a fine for dodging the fare.

Since my buddy and his partner were convincing as a game-show host and sidekick, the contestants would anxiously try to answer the questions posed to them with earnestness and sincerity, hoping to be categorized as a mope. The questions were rather simple, such as "Who's buried in Grant's Tomb?" One of the stock questions was, "Name five states," and often the answers were truly bizarre, such as, "Russia," "Chicago," and my favorite…, "*Up*-state."

On one particular instance, my buddy queried an aspiring mope, a short, somewhat nervous teenager wearing a leather jacket and slicked back hair. The question was, "When an apple fell from a tree, Newton called it 'gravity.' What is it when it falls from an apartment building?"

There was a long pause as the teenager thoughtfully took his time, bit his tongue, and then somewhat tentatively blurted out—"Gah-bage?"

Come on down, son! We have ourselves a mope!

Often, some of the cops stationed in the ballpark did their patrols on bicycles, which they left out in the basement corridor when they had to step into the station for police business. Since their station was near the vendor locker rooms, I was always amazed how the cops, for precautionary reasons, actually took the seats off their bikes to be sure they didn't get stolen. Were they afraid vendors would swipe these seats? I wondered what they thought of us for that to come into their consciousness. That's number one. Number two... They are cops. Even if that were to happen, they didn't have to *call* the cops—they are the cops!

The police station in the Yankee Stadium basement and the bikes

My family all grew up in New York, and my Uncle Abie, a former vendor himself with my dad back in the thirties, was one of its truest characters. Of Hungarian extraction, Abie was built exactly like my father—short and stocky. They were both about five foot nine, had a forty-two-inch waistline, wore thick-rimmed glasses, and were very opinionated.

Uncle Abie's brain was razor-sharp and his wit was even sharper. His generation thrived on sarcasm. He was my godfather, and I used to appreciate his comments, his words of wisdom, and his playful needling. One year, I was cast in a play, and I told him that the lead in the show, the producer of the play, happened to be a lousy actor—absolutely awful. His response was, "You say he's producing the play... He's the one paying for the production? Well, if you ask me, he's *The Greatest Actor In The World!*"

I was a notoriously big eater when I was kid. Still am, in fact, since my love for chicken has caused me to be called "A Chicken Magnet." My dad said my "eyes were bigger than my stomach," but my uncle would be a little more descriptive, as he used to say about me, "His knife and fork make sparks." He also said that I "only ate one meal a day... continuous!" He often told my mom her son "wouldn't eat 'til he was full, he would eat 'til his arms got tired." That was my uncle—a great New York character.

When I was about twelve or thirteen, I was playing in a Little League game, and Uncle Abie came to watch. Veterans Field in the Kingsbridge section of the Bronx was the best field I ever played on. Situated on the grounds of the Veterans Hospital, it actually had stands for family members to sit and watch the game from, something quite rare in the Bronx.

Most of my Little League games took place at large parks where baseball fields overlapped in the outfield and sometimes balls would roll from one game to another. Family and friends would bring folding chairs or stand along the foul lines to watch at those games, but at Veterans Field we played on a single diamond, complete with a fence around the outfield, which added a sense of significance. I had some great memories there, including once pitching a one-hitter at the age of eleven. Another game, I gave up a home run to George Grippo; my father joked the ball was still rising when it hit a building across the street.

On this particular day at Veteran's Field, my dad was working, so my uncle came for moral support, along with his son, my cousin Morty. I was catching, and there were a number of questionable calls from the home plate umpire against my team.

My uncle didn't stop razzing him with a few choice words from the stands, such as, "You're missing a good game, ump," or "I thought only horses slept standing up." Brutal. Clean, but brutal.

In the fourth inning, there was a close play at the plate. I made the tag, sure I'd gotten the guy, but the ump called him safe. My uncle went ballistic, came running onto the field, and got right in the ump's face. Uncle Abie was relentless. Clean, but relentless. In fact, the exchange was so heated, Uncle Abie was thrown out of the game.

Getting thrown out of a Little League game is not an easy thing to do, especially when you're sitting in the stands as a fan and not even in the game. But that's just what happened on this particular day, and Morty had to drive him away from the area. The ump actually refused to allow the game to continue until their car was off in the distance.

Once play resumed, the umpire, still puzzled from the interaction, asked me, "Who was that guy?"

For me, a scrappy little kid, I just took it that my Uncle Abie was a little opinionated and had a strong effect on people. "That's my uncle," I told him, never prouder of where I came from.

When Abie would talk to my dad, at a heightened decibel level, the conversation would invariably revolve around food—where to get the hot rolls with dinner, where to get the early bird special on the road, how to get "a deal." My uncle visited many of the national parks in his lifetime, and so he and my Aunt Annie did a lot of traveling by car in their day, therefore finding a lot of deals.

When Abie and my aunt would make their traditional Sunday visit to us he would sometimes explain to my father why they were late getting to our apartment:

"Construction woik on da highway. By da Deegan. Yeah... Dese construction guys on da road. They're always getting' *ready* ta woik. They're never really woikin'. They're havin' cawfee, they're lookin' at plans, smokin' a cigarette. Always gettin' *ready* ta woik... Never really woikin'."

One Sunday, my uncle and aunt came for a visit and brought an apple pie. Somewhere in the Old Testament it must be written that when Hebrews visit friends or relatives:

> Thou shalt always bring a box of Danish...
> or some equivalent.

When Abie and Annie were leaving, my mom told him to take back the pie, which hadn't even been touched, so they could snack on it for the long drive home to Washington D.C.

"No," my uncle grunted as he headed for the door. "That pie's for you."

My mother persisted and then, knowing my uncle very well, looked around the kitchen and said, "At least take this tin of cookies. They're stale."

Bam! He immediately halted in the doorway. "They're *stale*?" he asked. And with that, he took the cookies, gave my mom a hug, and my aunt and uncle were on their way.

Every time I see a tin of those Danish-style cookies or construction *woikas* on the highway, or even when I see an umpire at a game, I think of my uncle.

Uncle Abie

My dad, Abe's younger brother, was not afraid to say what was on *his* mind, either. He used to tell us kids:

"What I don't know ain't worth knowin'."

"What's mine is mine and what's yours is mine."

"Never quit a waiter's job on an empty stomach. Eat first...

Then quit."

"I know the Bronx like the back of my hand."

And he truly did know the Bronx, having grown up there and driven its streets for many years. But he also stubbornly thought he knew everywhere in the Tri-State Area that same way, which was unfortunate for us, his family. Frequently, we'd be lost in Jersey, and my mom and three older sisters would beg him, "Ask someone for directions—ANYONE."

He'd respond emphatically, "I know where I'm goin'. Just give me a minute. Let me get my bearings!" So we gave him a minute... or sixty... 'til he got his bearings.

On our family excursions, he often called out to pedestrians from the car, frustrated by the way they would aimlessly cross the street, paying no attention to traffic. He then would turn to us in the car and growl, "They walk, they walk, they walk." If he were here now I am sure he would add, "They text, they text, they text." Or, "They tweet, they tweet, they tweet."

My father grew up during the Depression, and whatever he learned back then about survival, he never forgot. Something expensive he called "telephone numbers," or he'd often say, "It's not a lot if you say it fast." When he was completely flummoxed by the absurdly high cost of something, he'd sarcastically say to me, "Buy *two*."

He also was the cook in our family, since my mother only knew how to make egg salad sandwiches—eggs and a little mayo—slapped between two slices of bread. My dad, like so many of his generation, was guided by his Depression-era mentality. His mother, my grandmother, used to bake wonderful, cinnamon-walnut cookies, which we grandkids would call "star cookies." Only years later did I find out she was only able to bring over one cookie cutter from Hungary when she migrated here and it was the one in the shape of a star.

If we had a little leftover chicken from dinner, the next day my dad would dice it into chicken chow mein, combining it with sautéed onions and celery. If he saw slightly bruised apples or peaches on sale at the supermarket, he would hack off the bad part and make fruit salad with the good. Nothing went to waste in our house.

When I was growing up with my three sisters, we lived in a three-bedroom apartment in the West Bronx, where the rent was $115 a month. When I was thirteen, we moved further north in the Bronx to another three-bedroom apartment but with a larger living room and a dining room; the rent skyrocketed to $248 a month.

With six mouths to feed in our family, those figures were not easy to come by on the first of the month, so our family phone bill was always a concern for my dad. This, of course, was before cell phones, so the home phone was a crucial element in a family's social life. One year back in the sixties, before push button phones, he actually put a lock on our landline phone. This locking apparatus was inserted into the rotary dial's first hole, which would then get stuck at the metal curved device or finger stop, preventing the faceplate from properly turning. No more ridiculous phone bills for him. He'd bellow to his family, starting with the Yiddish word for enough: "*Fartik*! That's *IT*! You can only make calls if they're related to schoolwork. Questions about your class, questions about your homework, *but that's it!*"

It was like a chastity belt for the phone. I actually spent much of that winter making my personal calls at a booth in our local subway station. From seven to eight every night, I would bring a pocketful of change and a can of soda with me to the phone booth and slink down onto the floor to talk to my friends. I only recently found out that one of my sisters' ways of dealing with the lock was by continually clicking the cradle of the phone until the operator came on the line. Then she would beg to have dialing assistance, because "I hurt my hand," or "I can't find the number," or—and I can't even believe this one myself—"I'm blind. Can you help me?"

Of course, the operator would help out. (Nowadays it's, "Press 1 for English, press 2 for Spanish," etc.) Back then, a teenage girl's desire to gossip took precedence over telling the truth.

A lock on the phone. I guess trying to feed a family of six by juggling three jobs at a time can do that to a person.

My father and I had our bonding moments for sure, though he never took me to a game at Yankee Stadium. He was a National League guy, so I went to Shea a few times with him to see the Mets in the late sixties. I also remember him taking me to see a football game at the Polo Grounds to see the Titans, who were the New York Jets before the Jets became the Jets. "You see that man with the football?" he'd say, squinting from our seats way up high in the grandstand. "That's the quarterback."

Back in the sixties, my dad also took me to the old Madison Square Garden at 49th Street and Eighth Avenue to see the Rangers play hockey. He would wear his multi-colored wool, Scottish beret (he even wore it to weddings, much to my mother's dismay), and we always sat in the side balcony, because the tickets were the least expensive at a dollar fifty each.

Unless seated in the first or second row, which were for season ticket holders and therefore difficult to acquire, we couldn't see half the ice and part of the game. The best seats we ever had were row "B," but usually we were in row "C" or "D" or higher, missing whatever happened on our side of the ice. The view from the end balcony was of the whole rink, but those tickets sold out quickly and were an exorbitant *two* dollars each, so we *never* sat there. I didn't mind, but I also recall that the end balcony seats were the ones I *wished* we had; I'd look at them with such reverence and envy, never for a minute dreaming of being downstairs... The seats downstairs were for *rich* people.

There was a Nedick's hot dog stand right at the entrance to the old Garden, but a tradition for us was to go to a place called Grant's on 42nd Street. It was like a large speakeasy where the men would get draft beers and I'd have a soda and a hot dog. The unique thing about this place was that the mustard was served in a large, multi-gallon jug and daubed onto the food with a large, crusty, wooden spoon. Hot dogs and hamburgers were the only thing on the menu—not that there was a menu—

served straight from an expansive grill.

My memory of those glorious times is like an old black-and-white movie: hordes of men with an occasional child sitting at communal tables, eating delicious fast food, with the strongest brown mustard imaginable. I only wish I could go there today, but, unfortunately, Grant's is simply a memory, open for business in my mind only.

My dad was rather stubborn about certain things, and that's why he took me to *his* dentist while my sisters all went to my *mother's* dentist. That seems kind of odd, now that I think about it, since a family usually has a *family* dentist.

My dad's guy, Dr. Stone, was peculiar, to say the least. His office on Creston Avenue in the Bronx doubled as his apartment, and it was a mess—stacks of client records strewn about; sloppy for someone's home, let alone a dentist's office. Since he saved on rent for his business (no assistant, no secretary, no nothing!), he only charged two dollars per filling and never ever used Novocain, at least never on me. Instead, when he was about to use his drill, Dr. Stone would start imitating birdcalls. He would do some strange whistles and then look around the room to get a laugh by distracting me, calling out, "What's that?" "Who's there?" Then he'd drill my teeth.

When I was in grade school, we were required to bring in a signed dentist's note stating we'd made our annual visit and our teeth were in good shape. I obviously dreaded going to Dr. Stone, so I managed to falsify my note for two or three years. I first got into the stadium by having a faked note, too, so I guess I started young at that sort of thing. Unfortunately, this particular dental-note forgery backfired on me, because, when I finally did get in to see Dr. Stone, I had accumulated seventeen cavities. This meant I had to make a trip to see him for nine weeks in a row, as he did his whippoorwill routine incessantly while drilling my mouth. Because of Dr. Stone, I hated the sight and sound of birds right up until my late teens (except for chicken, of course).

Growing up with three sisters, privacy and a sense of fair

play could be difficult at times, but my dad instilled in us certain principles of democracy. We had one television set in the house, so whoever was first to come into the living room where the TV was had *dibs* on what shows to watch. However, in order to keep the right to choose a show, the person whose TV it was needed to say, "TV's reserved," when they left the room.

The same provision came with the most comfortable chair, so one had to say, "Seat's reserved, TV's reserved" to keep full privileges. I often quietly sat in the living room and, as soon as one of my sisters who had the rights would leave but didn't make the call, I would scream, "Ha-ha! Seat's mine, TV's mine. You didn't say 'seat's reserved, TV's reserved.'"

Of course, all bets were off once my dad came into the room. His presence was like a nonverbal, "Scram!" and he proceeded to take the best chair and, of course, control of the TV. Master of his domain.

He truly *was* master of his domain, and that domain was his household. When I was a teenager, I wanted to go to every concert in New York and even a few in Philadelphia. And I felt I *had* to go because, I naively thought in my youthful delusion, if I didn't get there, the producers might actually have to cancel the performance. Of course, the shows went on, and sometimes even without me.

My dad had such an iron will that I had to carefully pick and choose when I would ask if I could go out of town to see the Who, Emerson, Lake & Palmer, or some other rock band. Often, when he was seated in his big, comfy recliner chair watching *The Ed Sullivan Show*, I would listen from just outside the living room for when a comedian would make an appearance on the show. When I heard Bob Newhart, Myron Cohen, or Alan King, I would come in right as my dad was laughing and ask for permission to go to the out-of-town concert. He was completely distracted and, as he laughed, would grant me consent with a wave of his hand, and I would gleefully hustle out the door.

Our traditional family holiday, Hanukah, was a wonderful celebration for eight days. The first four days were set aside for each of the children to bestow gifts to the family. The first night might be my turn to provide the gifts; then the next night would be my sister Barbara's turn; then Robin, then Janet. On the final four nights of the holiday, our parents would give their gifts to us. To have our presents spread out over the full eight days of the holiday was quite special. We kids appreciated the satisfaction in giving and seeing how well the gifts were received on a night when we ourselves didn't get anything. I look back on that tradition gratified that my parents taught us some valuable lessons about the meaning of the holiday.

One year, Barbara and I decided we wanted to have a Christmas tree in the house, even though we were Jewish. My dad didn't exactly *endorse* this idea, but he eventually allowed us to have a "Hanukah bush," though he refused to buy ornaments for it. Not a problem. Our neighborhood was "typical Bronx," populated with Irish bars, penny-candy stores, and Jewish delis. But, most importantly, there were six-story apartment buildings in the area and each of those buildings was usually decorated with Christmas trees on display in the lobby. With one of us keeping an eye out, the other would swipe some tinsel or a ball from the tree, then move on to the next building.

As I look back on our scheme, it's clear that stealing Christmas ornaments might be construed as wrong. But, on further examination, *Your Honor,* my sister and I were actually exhibiting a spiritual-minded sense of the holiday. "I look out for you and you look out for me." We didn't want to get caught. Is that so wrong?

My dad was always succinct in his quips. On the odd occurrence when we would bring home a good report card, he would always, and I mean *always,* review the grades and, in the little space for comments, write back to the teacher, "Room for improvement." On one occasion, one of my sisters brought back straight As, and he responded back with the comment, "Quite pleased. In fact... stunned!"

My dad was always hustling. When he was a kid in the thirties, he vended in the stadium and then, years later, my grandfather had a butcher shop on Eighth Avenue in Manhattan, so my dad worked there for many years. Then he moonlighted by driving a cab at night while also going to Fordham University to learn the insurance business. That was his "balancing act," I guess. He worked extremely hard, and he taught me to do the same. We had our battles, of course, but in retrospect, my relationship with him was close.

Every year, I had trouble figuring out what to get him for his birthday. Sometimes, I would simply be instructed by my mom to go into his closet and rewrap one of his ties. "He won't know the difference," she'd say.

As a kid, my gift-giving motives were sometimes self-serving, like when I got him a subscription to *Sports Illustrated*. In my teens, when I was working steadily at the stadium, one year for his birthday I told him to keep my $10-a-week allowance. I was off the dole. I think he liked that one.

He always tried his best to take us on a modest but fun family road trip each year to nearby places, like Gettysburg, Pennsylvania or Niagara Falls. I can still recall him prodding us like a drill sergeant to get into the car: "We're movin' out in columns of two." One year, we drove to Florida from New York, and he insisted we get a substantial start in the morning—"A hundred miles before breakfast."

In the early seventies, after he had earned his insurance license, I would often accompany him to his office, located in a small building next to Harlem's Apollo Theater. Pop would allow me to go to a nearby Muslim-owned bakery that sold loaves of delicious whole wheat bread while he went up to get his mail. I may have been the bakery's only white customer, but it didn't concern them or me; I was a regular and was always met with smiling faces from the colorfully turbaned women behind the counter. We'd share a kind word, and I would scoot out onto 125th Street, picking off pieces from the end of the loaf as I met up with my dad a block or two away.

When he made collections from his customers in some of the most dangerous neighborhoods in the city, from the South Bronx to Spanish Harlem, he'd double-park our Ford Valiant, and I would sit in the passenger seat so we wouldn't get a traffic ticket. He told me to "ride shotgun" as he scooted upstairs into an apartment building to pick up the premiums he would make a few dollars on. I guess commission has been a way of life in our family for a long time.

My dad was a quirky guy, no doubt about it. He was a chronic squeezer, whether it was melons at the supermarket to see if they were ripe, my cheeks... to drive me crazy, and even the back of new shoes. ("Ya gotta have support back there or your feet'll kill ya.")

He used to often proclaim, "I never used deodorant a day in my life." With that, my sisters and I pretended to hold our noses, looked at each other, and squealed, "We know, Dad, we know," but he really didn't smell bad.

And I still have nightmares from when I released the emergency brake on his car and rolled over my cousin's bicycle when I was six years old. My family was at my aunt's house, and he was having coffee in the living room when he looked out the window, saw me, and came running down the sloped front lawn with his arms flailing at his sides. The image of my dad coming down that hill was similar to when George Brett came charging out of the dugout when a pine tar technicality on his bat disallowed his home run in a game against the Yankees in the eighties. You can check it out on YouTube—that's just what my dad looked like that day.

Both my parents died relatively young—my mom was sixty-two and my dad only fifty-six. I was twenty-one when he passed away, and his death was a particularly significant moment for me, since I was still living at home in the Bronx when we found out he had liver cancer.

He lasted less than eight months from the time he was diagnosed, but he took his fate admirably well. In one quiet moment with my sister Robin, he whispered to her, "Let's face it... What machine lasts fifty-seven years?" My mom attended to him diligently, as he would beckon to have his back scratched or call adamantly for water or simply scream out for no reason at all. Since I was the only child still living at home, I witnessed his decline firsthand.

As anyone knows who has watched a relative or loved one die, it is heart wrenching to see someone strong and full of life be so weakened by an awful disease. He had been a stubborn, brazen individual who could turn to mush at the mention of his grandchildren's names. When he was bedridden towards the end, touching the hand of my sister Janet's children was the only thing that could make him smile, could actually make him feel better.

In his final few days, while he lay motionless in a coma, we tried to give him ice cubes and dabs of water from a napkin or Q-tip to keep his mouth hydrated. But we knew it was a losing battle. As the days wore on during that dreadful time, I was secretly wishing him to go. It was clear he wasn't going to recover, and it was very difficult for my mom to see him in that state. Each night, as I would pass his room, I'd check to see if he was still breathing.

On his last night I looked in on him and this time he *wasn't* breathing. My mom at that time had moved into another bedroom—she couldn't emotionally bear sleeping next to him anymore. Suddenly, I started to bang on his chest, begging for him to stay alive, all the while doing it as quietly as possible so as not to wake my mother in the other room. For days, I had hoped he would end his and her misery, but in this real moment I was praying for him to keep breathing. Unfortunately he didn't... and he died at approximately 2 a.m. on February 11, 1977.

I didn't know it until that morning, but when a body stops breathing, it's prone to defecate, so I had to deal with that, also as quietly as possible. I rolled him over, took off the sheets, cleaned him up, got fresh linen, and remade the bed. Then I took the soiled sheets down to the street to toss into the trash, all the while trying not to wake my mom.

For days leading up to his passing, I knew that I wanted to

write a eulogy for him. However, I couldn't do it, because it was impossible to think about him in the past tense, since he was still breathing and alive.

I had had a rocky relationship with him, for sure. After having three daughters, he seemed extra-strict with me, his only son, often hitting me with a strap when I didn't "toe the line," as he put it. Once, I overheard him comment to someone sarcastically that I was "trying to find myself" when I was struggling through my college years, unsure of which path I wanted to take with my life. Some phrases sting more than others, and that's one that hurt my adolescent ego.

My folks

He had truly been the master of our family—he reminded my sisters and me of that daily. I still feel his presence in my life when I think to myself, *Oh, Pop would have said this*, or, *my father used to say that all the time*. And I will never get out of my mind the image of him in the street in his bathrobe and slippers.

He had been called because I had been on my bike when I

was about eleven and ran a stop sign, getting hit by a car in the crosswalk. Turns out I was fine, a large bruise on my thigh that took a few visits to Dr. Ginsberg's, but luckily I was okay.

I was expecting my father to breathe fire on me because I messed up the bike. It was completely bent out of shape, never to be used again, a heap of junky metal. But he was concerned only about me. He came running out of the house, not even taking time to put on clothes, dressed in his robe and slippers. And he didn't put on his good robe: he hastily ran out in the navy-blue terry cloth one with the holes in it.

On his final morning, after I had cleaned him up and called one of my sisters to come up to be there for when my mom awoke, I was able to compose his eulogy. With a bit of assistance from Barbara, it poured out effortlessly as I sat at our kitchen table while the sun came up. I wrote of that gritty, hard-working, scrappy man who'd helped shape my life then and who still does now.

When I read the eulogy at his funeral, it was comforting for me to see his friends and family acknowledge with bowed heads when something rang true for them. And when all of us caravanned to the cemetery, a string of over seventy cars, my family did something I know my dad would have approved of.

Whenever he had someone follow him over a bridge or through a tunnel during a car trip, he always drove through the booth first and paid their toll. He loved looking back in his rearview mirror as his friend smiled at the modest but sincere token of generosity. So, for his funeral, our family pulled up to the booth in his hearse and paid the toll for all the cars in the procession. Seeing the smiles on the drivers' faces as they recognized the familiar gesture was quite special. My dad's peculiar little way of sharing had now become a family heirloom.

One story about my dad that captures him accurately is about the time he was scheduled to go to a Broadway show (my mom's idea, no doubt) immediately after his shift at my grandfather's butcher shop.

My father liked his big band music and would often hang out at my Uncle Mickey's record store in the neighborhood, so, on this night, he went over there for an hour or so before meeting up with my mom. While there, Evans, who worked for Mickey, politely mentioned that this was a "fancy-schmancy" Broadway theater he was going to, and he and his clothes reeked of, frankly, bloody, smelly meat.

My dad looked up at him and said, rather nonchalantly, "They'll take my money." Pride. Some might perhaps say arrogance, but blue collar to the bone. That was my dad.

My Uncle Mickey, on my mother's side, owned the record store and was another character in a city full of them. Mickey got into the record business and was actually in competition with his younger brother, Sammy, whose Record Haven shops grew to four stores in the metropolitan area to Mickey's one.

Sammy was the relative with the line that always gave us a laugh: "You'll never get out of this world alive." He also taught me ever so carefully how to use a peel of lemon to rim my glass whenever I had my Scotch on the rocks. I thought it was an odd little lesson to teach me, since I was only twelve at the time, but it served me well once I reached drinking age.

Mickey, a short, scruffy guy built like George Raft, was a terrific dancer. My mom told me that when they were growing up, he used to practice his moves with a dining room chair. "Became a real good hoofer that way," she said. He also was a bit of a gambler his whole life. When he died, after semi-retiring to Florida, his lucky red sports jacket was found in his closet with 7,000 dollars cash in its pockets.

Mickey's record store was in the subway station at 42nd Street and Eighth Avenue. In those days, shops in the subway corridors were very common—now, not as much. The store was a browser's delight, next to a barbershop, down the steps from the street; a place where one could rummage through record album covers in large bins.

I used to go when I was a kid. There was a hi-fi in the back where my uncle would allow people to sample selections before they purchased anything. My dad acquired most of his old jazz 78s from that store. He'd often come home with these large-scale, thick discs of Duke Ellington, The Mills Brothers, Benny Goodman, and many others. Also, some of the more eclectic artists, like Chu Berry, Erskine Hawkins, and one of the best vocal groups around, the Charioteers, doing a song called "Ride Red Ride." Once a month on a Sunday morning, when he would make us waffles in an old waffle iron, he'd put on those records and the house was rockin'.

Mickey had Evans, a middle-aged man who wore a stylish hat and always had a cigarette nearby, playing the records in the back. He looked a bit like Thelonious Monk, the great pianist, but most important, he had a wonderful attitude for life—smiles for miles. I used to love going there, a great place for people-watching, where mostly black, working class customers came in to sample some music and shoot the shit with Evans. It was an eclectic mix—even the champion prizefighter Emile Griffith was a regular.

There's a family story from the late thirties about a skinny kid who came into the store with a few eight-by-ten glossy pictures. Apparently he had just released a record and asked Evans if he could hang out and sign autographs, kind of a smalltime promotion-type thing. But my uncle overheard, and as far as he was concerned, the kid wasn't promoting. He was *loitering*. So Mickey went over to him and said, "Get lost. And take your friggin' pictures with you!" And that is the story of how my Uncle Mickey threw Frank Sinatra out into the street.

Years later, Mickey's son also got into the record business. When one of his steady customers asked for career advice, he told her never to sign with the Atlantic record label because, "You'll get lost over there." Lucky for her, and *us*, Bette Midler didn't take his suggestion. Clearly, my cousin had an acute eye for talent, just like his dad. How does that saying go—the acorn doesn't fall far from the...? Well, something like that.

It also reminds me of how wonderful New York is in terms

of seeing celebrities. One night, I was having a drink with a friend of mine, and I had *my* Sinatra moment.

In the forties, fifties, and sixties, 52nd Street was *THE* street for jazz. There was a string of nightclubs, and the musicians, some of whom worked in pit orchestras on Broadway, would hop from one joint to another to jam and sit in with their friends and colleagues. Charlie Parker started in those great clubs, as well as Miles Davis, Dizzy Gillespie, and Billie Holiday. By the time I went in the late seventies, there were only one or two clubs left; in fact, they had moved up to 54th street, yet there was still a great excitement to that area.

One time, I was at place called Jimmy Ryan's, leaning against the long bar, which led into where the bandstand and tables were. Suddenly, who should walk in, complete with a large entourage, but the same guy my uncle tossed years earlier... Frank Sinatra. I nudged my friend. "Hey! Look who's here."

And, incredibly, Sinatra appeared to be walking straight towards me! As he was about to brush by, I gathered my nerve and gulped, "*Uh*, how's it goin', Frank?"

Well, he and his entourage stopped dead in their tracks right there, and he gave me a series of looks. The first was the *Do-I-know-you?* look. The second, which came immediately afterwards, was the *I-don't-know-you* look. But then he said to me—he actually said to *me*—"How're ya doin', baby?" And then he kept on walking, *poof!* And vanished.

Maybe I never had my own TV series or won an Oscar and maybe I never will, but Frank Sinatra called me *baby*.

Years later, on another visit to a bar in New York (I like to drink, what can I say?), I met the enormously successful Pat Riley, who was coaching the Knicks at the time. I don't like to miss out on an opportunity, so I struck up a conversation.

Around that time, I had finished rehearsals for a play, which was still running in Los Angeles, so I asked him, "Pat, on any given night, the Knicks can lose to a lousy team. How do you keep them mentally up? I'm directing a play in Beverly Hills right now, and sometimes there aren't a lot of people in the audience. It's a pretty small theater, and the energy of the actors can get very low. What do I do?"

Riley, a hero of mine, got a fire percolating in his eye, and he stared me down. And he's stared down the best of 'em, from Magic to Kareem to Shaq. But this time, he stared *me* down.

"Let me ask you something. It's a ninety-nine-seat theater, right? (*Yup*) And you've got an audience of mostly old people, right? (*Yup*) And sometimes there are more people in the cast than in the theater, right? (*Yup*) Listen, you tell those actors that that is when they have to work harder. They have to speak up—louder, and dig in! You tell them to make their characters, their acting, their choices… clean… Strong!"

It was as if I was in a huddle with this master coach, and he was chewing me out, right in a bar on 89th and Third. It was great advice, and a week later, when I got back out to the theater, I kicked butt.

Of course, sometimes interactions with celebrities take a turn that can't be anticipated. There was a well-known club on 44th Street in the Hell's Kitchen area called The Improv, where comedians would perform as they were starting out. The major comedians who came out of that era, from Jay Leno, Rodney Dangerfield, and Robert Klein to Richard Pryor and Lily Tomlin all played there, sometimes doing their regular material and sometimes tweaking some new stuff.

One night, I was there with a friend, and it was very late. I'd say it was well past two in the morning, and my buddy and I and perhaps three or four other people were the only customers in the place. The final comic we were watching that night was Larry David, who would later, of course, become ultra-successful by co-creating *Seinfeld*. In the early eighties, however, he was a stand-up, and he was working on new material to this small gathering of listeners who were in various stages of inebriation.

During his set, he spent a lot of time conversing with us in the audience and, most specifically, to my friend and me. He was simply asking us questions, such as where we were from, just getting us into conversational mode, a give and take. At this late hour, with virtually no audience to speak of, he was probably looking to see if he might hatch a joke or two for a future bit.

My friend and I were actually pretty funny, trading barbs with David and, in fact, making him crack up and laugh out loud. Maybe it was the alcohol, but I honestly thought we were funnier than he was—in fact, a lot funnier.

Larry David, unfortunately, as anyone can attest who has seen his persona on his own show, *Curb Your Enthusiasm*, can be somewhat caustic. And this was early Larry, when he hadn't fully honed that character that, later, would have the sarcastic edge that made him so sharp and witty. I love the later Larry, but on this night, I didn't really care for his pointed shtick. Not one bit.

We soon started snipping at one another, and he became rather rude and condescending, so I tossed it right back at him. I'd eventually had enough and told my friend I would wait back in the bar 'til the set was finished.

Turns out it didn't take long for David to sign off. My friend came and met me for another beer. Then David came back, as well, sat on a stool, and ordered a club soda. After a tense moment or two, since we were the only ones in the vicinity, my friend was feeling a little conciliatory and he appealed to me, "You were pretty rough on him. Why don't you go over and tell him you're sorry?"

Frankly, I didn't have anything to feel sorry about. But I thought, oh why not? So I went over to apologize. Or at least I started to. "Hey, listen. I'm sorry what happened in there, but...." And I tried to come up with just the right words. I really did. I wanted to make myself absolutely perfectly clear, I really did. But it came out, "I'm sorry... but... let's face it... You got no act."

For some reason, Larry David didn't care for my critique

and, at that point, slid off his stool, looked me right in the eye, and said rather bluntly, "Fuck you!"

I was shocked, not by what he said but how simplistic it truly was, so I came back with, "Is that all you got...? Really?"

My friend, who is 6'3" and not afraid to let everyone know it, got between us, and, thankfully, the moment ended peacefully. As time went on and Larry David's career went through the roof, I have often thought back to that early morning on 44th Street, when he had the weakest of retorts to my drunken heckle.

Who knows, perhaps our encounter made him realize he wasn't cut out for stand-up and was better off going to Hollywood and getting behind the scenes as a producer. Hey, Larry! If you're listening... You owe me.

And as a follow up to that, I saw an episode of *Curb Your Enthusiasm* where Larry was cast in a movie playing an Italian mobster, complete with a bad toupée and a hard-edged attitude. His friend in the show, Richard Lewis, asked him, "How did you get this part as a Godfather type? It's not believable—you can't act."

David looked at him and said, "Scorsese once saw me at a club and loved how I handled a heckler, so he cast me in the film." I almost fell over—I thought he was talking about me!

New York never fails to surprise me. It's where I can stroll into my local Xerox shop and see a homeless man on a computer, downloading his memoirs. Or I can go to a pizza place for the best slice in the city, and it's made by a guy from Croatia. Or take a subway ride and be entertained by a magician who actually has two live doves in his act, right there on the D train. In fact, I have seen numerous dog acts on the subway, a man doing the tango with a fully dressed doll sewn onto his suit jacket's shoulder, one-man bands and eight-man bands, classical violinists, jazz troupes from Sweden, and any number of other elaborate and professional acts. "All I have are my skills, to pay my bills," says one of them. One doesn't need money to be entertained in New York, just a MetroCard.

And where else can I see another man near the subway entrance sitting in a wheelchair with a cup, begging for donations while smoking a cigar? I sometimes think he has the cup out so he can get enough money to buy himself a little cognac to go with the cigar.

New Yorkers don't care for small talk. Once, I went to a memorial for the great playwright Arthur Miller. When someone of his stature dies in New York, there is usually a memorial service the public is invited to attend. On this particular day, I was leaving the Broadway theatre where the event was being held, and I caught a glimpse of Lauren Bacall right in front of me. Just then, a middle-aged woman came rushing up to her and said, "Are you Lauren Bacall?"

And she responded, with impeccable timing, "Well who the hell do you *think* I am?"

Only in New York can one see people begging with pure honesty, carrying a sign, "Let's Face It, I Need a Beer." Or another with a sign and a smile that says, "Please Give to the United Negro Pizza Fund." Once, a homeless man asked an old girlfriend of mine if she could spare a cigarette. She told him, almost apologetically, "I only have Virginia Slims," to which he replied, as he took one, "Hey, beggars can't be choosers."

Occasionally, there are side businesses and moneymakers that emerge via my fellow vendors, often right in the locker room. The year Michael Jackson died, one vendor was selling posters of him for a buck. Many have sold bootleg DVDs or replica baseball caps in the locker room to their co-workers. There always seemed to be some kind of venture popping up, just like when Wilson was selling The Duke football when I started vending those many years ago.

One season, after the Yanks had won the World Series, a fellow vendor asked me if I wanted to sell pennants at the parade hosted for the team near Wall Street, down the infamous "Canyon of Heroes." This is always a raucous event, a celebration that has the real hardcore fans lining the street to cheer on the world champions, whether they are the Yankees,

Mets, Giants, Jets, Knicks, or Rangers.

The plan was for me to pick up some items from a car near the area and stroll through the crowd, selling championship pennants. Then I would return to the car, replenish my stock, and carry on until the two-hour parade ended.

As I was doing my business, a tough-looking female cop motioned for me to come over to where she was. I had been warned to be careful, because the police could confiscate my stuff, so I walked toward her with great trepidation. My imagination was swirling, as I couldn't help but think how much money I was about to lose by her taking my souvenirs or writing me a summons.

When I got up to her, she looked at me sternly and, pointing to a nearby ten-year-old, said, "I think this kid wants to buy a pennant."

I mean, come on. Ya' gotta love this town.

POCKET MONEY

WHEN I STARTED working in Yankee Stadium in 1970, I was only fifteen years old, a pimply-faced kid in high school. The job was perfect for me: part-time, and a way to secure "pocket money," as my dad used to call it.

Over the years, like most people, I've had, various types of jobs to help me get through school or to pay the rent. I skipped a grade in junior high and the high school I went to in the Bronx was Dewitt Clinton, an all-boys school where many of those boys majored in *bullying*. It wasn't unusual to be harassed at lunchtime by the bigger, older kids who would say to me, "Can I hold a quarter?" When I said I didn't have one, the common response was, "All I find I keep?"

I also got randomly punched during pranks such as "Open Chest Week," when the bigger students hit the smaller ones, like me, at will. I wanted to get away from Clinton as fast as possible, and I managed to get a job in a stationery store through a connection from my mother.

I used to stock shelves and make deliveries for this little shop near the Empire State Building in Manhattan. The owner was an eighty-three-year-old, white-haired man named Mr. Lanz, who, most of the time, had an old-fashioned nickel cigar hanging from his lip. After years of smoking, this lower lip hung down like a small shelf protruding out just a wee bit for his cigar to settle on, not unlike the way a little trough is molded into an ashtray. When he took the cigar out of his mouth, the indentation on his lip remained. Seventy years of smoking will do that.

A few days a week after school, I would go down to the store at 30th Street and Sixth Avenue, which was around the corner from where Macy's holds its Thanksgiving Day Parade. Depending on my class schedule, I would stock shelves and make local deliveries from either two to six or three to six in the afternoon. At the end of my workday, Mr. Lanz would ask me what time I came in. I would tell him, and he would then pay me just before I left to go home. At two dollars an hour, he gave me either six dollars or eight dollars each day. He'd put his cigar down on the edge of a counter, take out a large wad of money wrapped in a thick rubber band, and count out my pay. I would stuff the bills in my pocket and head to the subway and back up to the Bronx.

The shop had a "Norman Rockwell" feel to it: all wood trim from the early part of the twentieth century, and it had ladders that slid along a railing. Mr. Lanz was somewhat frail, but he was also stubborn and fearless. He loved to climb up to get anything a customer might need, even something as small as a box of thumbtacks or paper clips.

I would often come in and, upon seeing him up there, call out, "Mr. Lanz, Mr. Lanz! Let me get that for you."

He'd blow a puff of smoke and reluctantly climb down the ladder, a little disappointed he had been relieved of his errand and the fun of being ten feet in the air.

There used to be an old-time hat shop on Sixth Avenue in the vicinity of Mr. Lanz's store, and I would longingly stare in the window whenever I walked to and from the subway. I had my eye on a hat, a sky-blue Cuban fedora, and after weeks of saving up my salary, I went in and treated myself. It was thirty bucks, which took me quite a while to accumulate, but I bought it, and whenever I wore it, my Spanish seemed to improve—a *very* Cuban hat. That was part of my early education in saving my own money for something I wanted.

The neighborhood where I lived in the West Bronx was near Featherbed Lane, which was a long distance from the shopping district and nearest grocery store. For that reason, some of the apartment buildings in the area installed milk machines in the basement where one could get quarts of fresh cold milk, thereby allowing the tenants the ability to avoid the inconvenience of hiking a mile or more to the closest supermarket. My dad would often give me two quarters, point to the door, and bark, "Go across the street and get two milk."

The quarts of milk at the time were twenty-three cents, and I would get to keep the pennies. So there it is—my first commission was at eight percent, a total of four cents. Cash!

On one of these occasions when I was fetching some milk, I reached into the coin slot for the two cents change, and I dropped a penny onto the ground. I got down on my knees and felt around under the machine for what had fallen. The building's basement was dark, dusty, filthy, yucky, but what do you know? I found a dime under there. But finding that dime turned out to be a mixed blessing.

The best thing about finding money is, "Wow! I just found some money." The worst thing is, by continuing to look, I thought I could find *more* money. But rarely does that hold true, and I can vouch for the fact that it doesn't happen very often underneath milk machines. How do I know this? Because, for the rest of my childhood, so long as we still lived in that neighborhood, when I would get some milk, I would also crouch down on my knees to feel around for more lost change. In my experience, which was approximately six years of milk fetching, from when I was eight to when I was thirteen, I can unequivocally state it's not an effective use of one's time. I probably found a total of no more than eighty-five cents over the next six years.

As time went on, I came up with easier ways to find money. One Halloween, I went to an apartment building a few blocks from my house, and someone in 3B gave me a quarter—I guess they didn't have any candy and were giving out money instead.

Since a quarter to a nine-year-old was equivalent to a million dollars, I came up with a plan. I figured I would run home and change my costume.

A 1958 family (l to r: Janet, me, my dad, Robin, my mom, Barbara)

When I was growing up, my mom always dressed me up as a "supermarket," defined simply by an old white sheet with a hole in the center for my head and items pinned on, such as empty boxes of cereal, cookies, and soap detergent. I was essentially wearing garbage, all there to replicate a... voila...! "supermarket," the Halloween costume I was sent out in every friggin' year. She couldn't make a home-cooked meal, but she always made a "home-made" costume.

So I ran back to our apartment and, with the help of my sister Robin, we moved the boxes around on my sheet (Rice Krispies box switched to the back, Chips Ahoy to the front) and proceeded to head back to 3B. It worked! Fifty cents in one night, not to mention all the candy I could eat from everyone else in the neighborhood. Now that I think about it, that was probably my first paying gig as a performer, playing the role of a "supermarket."

When I was a teenager, I had many jobs: everything from handing out flyers in the city for a massage parlor called "Relaxation Plus" (I never found out what the "plus" stood for, but I can just imagine) to driving around the Bronx selling uniform jackets to barbers and beauticians. Someone in my family knew somebody who had a connection in the garment district. I would roam around, walk into a beautician's shop, show my stuff, and sell some jackets for six dollars apiece. I think I made a dollar fifty a jacket.

When I was going to acting school, I also had a waiter's job in a luncheonette on Madison Avenue. I would often work the breakfast and lunch shift, which went from 7 a.m. to 2 p.m. My classes at that time started at two, so my boss graciously let me check out at ten to two. Then I would go running down Madison Avenue from 40th Street to 30th Street, brushing by hordes of New Yorkers, to get to class on time.

The extra money I had in my pocket was very welcome. One of my fellow acting students didn't have a job, and I would often see him swipe packets of sugar from the coffee shop across the street from the school so he could make sugar sandwiches for his snack break in the afternoon. Sometimes, he made ketchup sandwiches from little packets. Fortunately, he was a good actor, and, years later, when he had a regular part on a sitcom, we would laugh about it in his dressing room on the studio lot in Hollywood, a true "rags to riches" story.

My father sold insurance, and he would make extra money doing tax returns for some of his customers. When he had some of the easier short forms, he would let me do those and pay me three dollars apiece. He made two bucks subcontracting to me for each one, but I didn't mind. He deserved the commission.

Major League baseball players went on strike in 1981, and I had to scramble for money, so I got a job selling nuts off of a cart on Fifth Avenue. I had to go to the West Side of Manhattan and weigh out my stock of various candies, dried fruits, and nuts, so I knew the total weight of what I started with. Then I would push the cart cross-town, find a spot frequented by pedestrians near St. Patrick's Cathedral, and stand there for about ten hours. That job lasted exactly one day.

The reason I quit was, when someone bought, for instance, a quarter pound of cashews or pistachios, I would toss in a few extra. Hey, it was cold, the scale I had was not exactly precise, and some of those teenage tourist girls shopping on the avenue were kinda cute. When I came back to the warehouse at the end of the day to check out, I was told by my supervisor that I had apparently given away quite a bit of nuts. So many, in fact, that when I did my tabulations, I ended up making a grand total of sixteen dollars for my ten-hour day. And I don't even want to mention how tough it was to hold it in when I had to go the bathroom. What could I do, go into a store and leave my nuts out to be stolen?

Having to hold it in reminds me of when I had my souvenir stand and needed to go during the course of a game. I would often feel chained to my inventory, patiently waiting for a familiar face to come strolling by. When I would see a fellow vendor or usher whom I knew I could trust, I would politely ask if they could "mind the store" as I made a quick dash to the nearest john. Many a hot, sweltering day I would forego having a cold drink simply because I realized I would eventually be at the mercy of my bladder. Those moments were often quite stressful, as I'd exhibit some fancy dance moves, looking longingly down every hallway and corridor for a familiar, trusting face.

My first few years at the ballpark, my seniority was low, meaning I didn't get the really profitable items to sell. In addition, during 1973-74, Yankee Stadium was being renovated, so the team played at Shea Stadium in front of very small crowds. During those years, I would often go to the Catskill Mountains to be a waiter or busboy at the various hotels up there. All of them are gone now, but I was on the payroll at the

Brickman's, Grossinger's, the Windsor, the Avon Lodge, Brown's Hotel, the Home-a-Wac, Gilbert's, the Raleigh, the DeVille, and many more. I used to say they had to build more hotels for me to work in, since I got fired from every one. There have been many stories documented about working in those hotels from the early forties and fifties, when Jerry Lewis, Danny Kaye, Sid Caesar, and countless others got their start entertaining in what was then known as the "Borscht Belt." The hotels were situated about a hundred miles north of New York City, and teenagers like me would work in the dining rooms, serving the guests three meals a day. They stayed for a weekend, a week, or the whole summer, and we lived on the tips we would receive at the end of their stay.

Unfortunately, we as staff would not eat nearly as well as the guests. We would be given leftovers: management saved money offering us second-rate food from the previous day's menu while serving top of the line for their guests. It seemed as if all we would get was either chicken or fish. I recall one employee, an Englishman with a summer work visa, who waited on line for his food and grumbled, "They keep this up, we're gonna grow bloody fins or wings." We employees felt the owners were showing their contempt for us by feeding us leftovers, even though it was simply prudent business on their part to cut corners when they could.

One job I had was at the Concord, at the time one of the very best resorts in the Catskills. All of the hotels were known for their gourmet food as well as various luxuries for the guests to indulge in, such as spacious swimming pools, golf courses, and other amenities that are now considered commonplace but back then were special. The Concord also used to book the top-name acts for their nightclub. Every year, they would host the likes of Don Rickles, Liza Minelli, Tony Bennett, and many others as a draw, similar to the way Las Vegas resorts do now. The people who were staying in nearby bungalow colonies, small summer-home rental properties, would often get dressed up in their finest formal wear, sneak onto the grounds, and bribe a maître d' in the nightclub, to see these performers.

One summer, I was a lifeguard at the Concord, even though I had never passed my Red Cross CPR test (not sure how I pulled that one off). Soon, I became friendly with one of the security guards who sat by the golf course on Saturday nights and watched as these well-dressed freeloaders tiptoed in to get to the nightclub. There was an opening in the fence by the eighth hole, and he would park himself near the green with a six-pack of beer and a garden hose. Bungalow colonies seemed to *breed* old people, and as these folks would be sneaking in, quietly whispering advice to each other on how to pull off their covert operation, he would hose them down 'til they were drenched, having a great laugh at their expense. When I asked him why the Concord didn't fix the fence, he replied with a grin, "Are you kiddin'? Over my dead body."

Saturday night in the Catskills was traditionally roast beef night. One year I found myself at a hotel just outside of Monticello, and they put me up with some other waiters in a house with a Boy Scout troop. After staying a whole summer with these Scouts, my fellow waiters devised a plan to sneak some roast beef out of the dining room for the troop of twelve. This was our version of *Ocean's Eleven*, trying to outfox our maître d', Mr. G. (short for Ginsburg, Goldberg, or Goldstein—I forgot which), who was a tyrant and always seemed to be looking to fire his staff based on the weakest of excuses.

We had a great plan—Operation Boy Scout, so to speak. Three waiters and three busboys would order one or two extra roast beef dinners on each trip to the kitchen. Once he returned to the serving station, the busboy would open a drawer and stack the meat on a linen napkin while putting the accompanying French fries in another drawer where the silverware was kept. When each waiter had four servings, the meat was transferred to another bus boy hiding behind the drapes near one of the dining room's windows. This in itself was difficult, as, on roast beef night, the portions were carefully counted; we slipped the kitchen's shop steward a few bucks to help us in Operation Boy Scout.

The bus boy behind the drapes, *me,* opened the window slightly for the final phase of the big heist. After our shift was over later that night, a couple of waiters came back onto the grounds with two of the most nimble Scouts. Since the dining room was on the second floor, getting to the crack in the window about ten feet off the ground was difficult. At this point, one of the waiters boosted one of the boys up, leaving the other Scout on the lookout while the second waiter loaded our booty into a shopping bag.

Of course, I realize we were stealing, and, perhaps even worse, we were enlisting the help of some adolescent boys in our scheme. *Boy Scouts* no less. But watching our troop members that night, all beaming with satisfaction at a plate full of roast beef and French fries, their best meal of the summer, somehow made it all worthwhile.

Another of my part-time off-season jobs was with a friend who had a video camera before they were popular. He would get work for both of us shooting weddings and bar mitzvahs all around the Tri-State Area. The cameras at the time were not as sophisticated as they are today, and he would often enlist me to hold lights so he could get good, clear footage.

One of his standard shots was of the elaborate smorgasbord display, the kind with various crudités, Swedish meatballs, "pigs in the blanket," and, of course, traditional chopped liver molded into the shape of Israel. Since we would be allowed to partake of some food during this cocktail hour, he would always tell me, "First, we shoot it. Then, we eat it."

Getting acting work has always been a huge challenge for me. It may take as many as forty auditions to land one job, something my fellow vendors didn't seem to understand. They were always quizzing me about this job and that, wondering why I hadn't booked the big career-making gig that would move them up on the seniority list. But they did take an interest with a sense of humor. One year, I booked a job on *Law and Order.*

When I told one of the guys I was playing a detective who found a body in the Hudson River, his response was, "Fishing a body out of the river, huh, Stew? What are they paying you... *scale*?"

But every year, when I would have to scrounge for extra "pocket money," I would always look forward to April, when the baseball season would once again begin and I would be back in Yankee Stadium. With my magnet schedule placed prominently on my refrigerator or a pocket schedule Scotch taped into my datebook or stashed in my wallet, I would know exactly where I would be for the next six months, affording a sense of structure to my somewhat sane life.

A vendor's bible; a schedule

In fact, all of my friends and family knew where I was simply by checking their newspapers to see if the Yankees were home. I used to say, "If the Yanks are in town, I'm in town."

HOW TO BE A GOOD VENDOR

IF YOU EVER GET the chance to become a vendor (hey, ya never know), here are some tips for success:

Be courteous to the fans. This is crucial. Unless a fan wants what you have, you're in their way. And if you *do* have what they want, they want it *fast*, and then they want you *gone*. In addition, when they have something to say, they are rarely civil, especially when the Yanks are losing.

"Yo...@! Move!"

"Hey, get outta the way."

"What's goin' on here...? LET'S GO!"

"Hey, I didn't pay (fill in the blank) bucks to watch you, pal."

It is often worse than that, with a few expletives or a thrown peanut or two added for emphasis. And through it all, it's crucial that vendors avoid talking back. When I was younger, an older worker told me the old adage, "The customer is always right... especially when they're wrong."

Sometimes, a fan may order a beer and then doesn't pay attention when getting their change. Try not to take it personally, because, after all, they are there primarily to watch the game. Just gently slide the money into their hand, even if they aren't seeing it done, because they will feel it. And the same is true with the item you are selling them, whether it's peanuts, a hot dog, or a beer. Just place it, or gently shove it, into their hands and move on.

It can be challenging at times, but resist the urge to curse in front of, or at, the fans. Since customers often like to play around with vendors it's essential to maintain composure. Fans often think they're funny when they call out for a vendor and then immediately turn away once the vendor hears the call. It can be frustrating when they play these dirty tricks. One beer vendor got right up into the face of a culprit who thought he was being cute and said, "Now, what on Earth can possibly give you the impression that I am the fucking Cracker Jack guy?"

Funny? Yes. Good for business? No.

Save your energy. Since there are eighty-one scheduled games during the course of a season, it's important to be at your best. Walking up and down the aisles can be hard work on the body, and so it's necessary to be in optimum health in order to be successful. Being able to sell an extra bin of hot dogs a night can lead to a fifteen- to twenty-five per cent increase in sales. When the Yankees are in the middle of a long homestand, get your rest, so you can make enough money to afford to do what you want, once they go on the road.

Working the three hours or so of a game can be exhausting. To save some needed energy, put your tray or bin down on a railing whenever you can to avoid reaching all the way down to the floor. I usually found an empty seat, took out a beer or two to hold up to the fans, caught my breath for a moment, and gave my call. Another tactic is to put the tray on the ground halfway down the aisle and go the rest of the way with two beers in hand to flash to the crowd, the less lugging of the tray the better. Just don't lose sight of your product that you've left halfway up, since fans have a tendency to dip their mitts in there, if you know what I mean.

As I reached fifty, every physical maneuver I made during

the course of a game became a little bit more strenuous. When making a sale, I put the tray down a step above where I was in the stands, to save a few inches when I bent back down to retrieve it. Or I would lean part of the tray or bin on my foot, so the reach downward was an inch or two less taxing. It's only an inch, but multiply that by a hundred or more individual sales per game, and that's a lot of inches.

Years ago, we used to work regular doubleheaders, two games for the price of one. This was an inducement to get fans to come out to the ballpark, the same way the Knicks tried to get attendance up years ago with their doubleheaders in the sixties. Now the Yankees sell out many of their games, so when there is a rainout early in the season, the team sometimes reschedules a night game on the same day that the rained-out team is back in town. This is known as a day/night doubleheader. The first game starts at 1 and is usually over by 4:30. The place is then cleared out, and new fans arrive, paying a separate admission, for the second game, which starts at 7. This is tougher on the vendors, as it becomes a long and, for many of the old-timers, strenuous day. In between games, while the sweepers clean up, the vendors hang out or go for a meal, trying their best to conserve energy for the evening game, known as the "nightcap."

When the Yankees have a day game after a late night game, some of the vendors who have a long commute have been known to sleep at the ballpark somewhere... Not sure where. One told me he would sometimes go down to the field and use a grounds crew hose to take a "bachelor shower," a mini-spray here and there, in the morning, prior to that day's batting practice.

I have worked games when it's been as hot as 105 degrees, watching sweat pour down the bill of my cap right in front of my face. I have also seen fans carried out of the ballpark from dehydration. Some vendors keep a wet rag or towel tucked under their hat. I had taken to the habit of wearing wristbands with an ice cube tucked inside, to keep my veins cool. Sometimes, I even put ice cubes in my socks, which helped as well.

During a long homestand, I had my wet work clothes draped all around my apartment to dry out before I tossed them in the hamper. During hot spells in July and August my clothes sometimes took two days to dry before I could even wash them at my local laundromat! Often, my place looked like a men's locker room, with T-shirts and sweat socks hanging everywhere in sight.

When I got home after a hot day of work, I often iced it all down. As I got older, my muscles tended to cramp up more. Not fun. Those ninety-plus-degree days last long into the night. More not fun.

Look good. It's important to keep up your appearance, which means straighten your hat, don't let your shirt hang out, and keep pants at a manageable length. Unless selling souvenirs, stadium vendors are in the food business, and people don't want to be served food by someone who appears to be hygienically challenged. Some vendors, truth be told, *are* hygienically challenged. One even goes by the nickname "Stinky." To prevent getting a moniker such as that, it's important to exchange uniform shirts and hats in the linen room for fresh ones as often as the company will allow.

One game, a vendor on line in front of me had a huge horsefly sitting on his shoulder. From the time we were on that line until we checked in and then went down to the locker room, this fly did not move—it was there a good five or six minutes. In fact, the fly may still be on this guy's shoulder, and, really, why would it leave? Licking old doubleheader sweat, crusty mustard stains, and dried up cotton candy particles—a feast for a king, let alone a fly.

My advice: take a shower. As a vendor, you want to attract customers, not flies.

Know the trade. My experience as an actor has taught me about vocal projection. It is important to avoid using only head voice while vending. Communication is essential, and if you sound tinny, people way up in the back row will not hear the call. Breathe deep and, if possible, bellow. If the fans don't know what you're selling, you won't sell anything.

With items such as hot dogs or pretzels, a vendor is required to use a napkin or waxed paper before touching the product. Back in the '80s, this was referred to as the barrier law. I don't even know if it was an actual "law," but we were required to have a barrier between our hands and the edible item. Now, most food vendors wear plastic gloves, but I don't think that is sufficient. Someone can wear plastic gloves and scratch behind their ear all day long and the gloves will get dirty and unsanitary. When serving and, for that matter, when being served, always look for that barrier between the fingers and the food.

Amidst the mayhem that is a Yankee game, there is nothing that is obvious. That's why it's important, if you are selling ice cream cups, double check and don't leave the station without spoons or napkins. If selling hot dogs, stick your hand in there and grab a bunch of ketchup and mustard packets before heading out of the commissary. Sounds obvious, but the station gets extremely hectic with yelling, screaming, and horsing around, and it can be a long walk back when, selling your first dog, you realize you forgot the mustard. Back when we sold egg rolls (yes, we sold egg rolls), if I forgot the duck sauce, I had "a lot of 'splainin' to do."

I haven't poured beer from a can or bottle in many years, but I know that some vendors still do—Citi Field vendors, for instance. I used to have an oversized can opener, large enough to open an oil can with one swoosh, and I'd often come home with cuts and nicks on my fingers from hastily opening as many as two hundred cans during a game. The best way to pour from a can or bottle is to tilt the cup slightly, so the head created by the foamy beer is lessened. When I was pouring, it was vital for me to get the beer into the cup as efficiently as I could, so as to move on to the next customer. Don't rush. Do it right the first time, and you won't have to wait precious seconds for the foam to decrease to finish pouring the contents from the can. As far as sticking a finger into the foamed head to slow it down—I never did it, never will, and cannot vouch for its effectiveness. See barrier law, above.

To keep the peace with fellow vendors, there is an unwritten code that we don't go up someone else's aisle when they are selling the same item. That makes sense. Go the other way. There will be fans seated down a different section, not bombarded by vendors, who will be more receptive to buying than the fans seated in the area that has two vendors in their aisle.

An aisle I made a living on

Take care of your money. Usually, the first couple of sales will not be paid with exact change but with a twenty, before fans have had a chance to receive smaller bills from other transactions. If starting with a cash bank of only fifty dollars, you may have a fistful of twenties before you've finished selling the item's first load. Then you are forced to ask the fans for exact change, thus slowing down the pace or even potentially losing sales when they are unable to oblige.

Of course, if three people in a row need to break a hundred

dollar bill, that may be a problem, but that's rare. Bring enough cash to go to the money room before the game and get just what you need. I usually started with 150 dollars: fifty in singles and maybe seven tens and six fives. As the game continues, keep track, so you can replenish bills at the station as necessary. A vendor hates to lose a sale, especially on slow days, simply because he or she doesn't have the correct change.

On the subject of change, it's a good idea to separate money in your apron the same way every time you work. As an example, if the apron has three pouches, keep quarters in the middle, singles on the left side, and fives, tens, and twenties on the right. Just do whatever works. Some guys keep the fives with the ones; some guys put fifties and hundreds in their pants pockets, completely apart from the rest. The point is do whatever is comfortable for you, since you are accountable for whatever mistakes you might make, so don't forget that. In my stack of bills, I kept whatever the customer gave me on the outside, so I could simply take a peek at the last bill in case of a dispute. It can get crazy out there, and anything that helps the night go without incident, the better.

Be wary of counterfeit bills. At least twice a season, I would come back to the station after selling a tray and hear the warning from the checker: "There're some bad fifties out there tonight." Counterfeit bills often have a strange texture or an odd-looking pink tone, but if you collect a bad bill and turn it in at the end of the night, that bill may be confiscated, and you're out of luck for the money. No questions. That's it. So be wary of false bills. They can be lurking anywhere.

When you count your money, be aware that someone is probably watching. It *is* the Bronx, after all, but, more importantly it *is* money, and until you turn it in, *you* are responsible for it—all of it.

When I had my souvenir stand, I would look in each direction and duck behind some cardboard boxes or get down very low behind some kind of screen, to be out of anyone's vision before tallying up. When I was selling in the stands, I never counted my money in the seats; I would wait until I got back to the station and do it there.

Bills often get wet when vending. When I used to pour beer from cans, the bills would get soaked by the time I finished my first tray, and then they had a tendency to stick together. Be careful. Again, if you give out the wrong change because of it, you are responsible for your error.

Remember your customers. If I sold two beers to some fans in section twelve in the first inning, I'd try to come back to them in the third inning and say, "You guys ready?" If timed right, you can get repeat business, and, as any successful businessman or woman will tell you, there's no business like repeat business. When sales are slow, this tactic is very important. The fan will appreciate that you remembered them, and the service will seem personal, which, in fact, it is.

If you spot some fans just getting to their seats for the first time, walk right over to them. "Need a beer, guys?" They will think it serendipitous, often saying, "Hey, perfect—here's the beer guy," but you were simply eying their path, anticipating their needs, and hustling a sale.

In the old stadium, sometimes I might be fortunate to get "a group." Before asking for ID became the strict policy, I could sell as many beers as I wanted to one person. Often, I would be able to sell my whole case to someone who might be buying for his co-workers, who were sitting in one section for a company outing. I would simply unload twenty-four beers right under a seat, get my money, and move on. Ooh, I mi$$ those days.

So that I could be assured the customer buying the whole case would be faithful to me for the rest of the night, I would often give the buyer a break, letting him or her have a free beer or two on me. While I cut my profit for that particular sale, it was usually worth it, since he or she would look for me for the rest of the night. Any businessman would do the same. The password is volume.

One other thing: keep an eye on the game. If a Yankee hits a homer, the place goes crazy, and it's a good time to park the beer tray right in front of a group who looks like they might want to use the home run as an excuse to buy a round. When the mood is good, business is good. Be in the right place at the right time, change your call to "Celebrate!" and sales will undoubtedly increase.

Time is money. Over the years, I have been privileged to see many veterans at Yankee Stadium, including those from Iraq, Afghanistan, Kuwait, Vietnam, and World War II vets, like the Tuskegee Airmen Division, the first African-American pilots in US military history. I have seen the first pitch thrown out by men and women who may have lost their arms and/or legs in combat but who never lost their bravery or pride. It was always a humbling sight for me to witness these American heroes out on the pitcher's mound, and I always stopped working whenever a veteran threw out a first pitch.

I have worked more than 2500 games, and the national anthem was played before every one of them started. When it came to the anthem, I often tried to get back to the station while it was being sung, so I could continue working as opposed to stopping and standing still. I would pay for a tray, have a drink of water, and get some singles, but I kept working.

In my years of hearing anthems, I would say Chuck Mangione's rendering was exhilarating, José Feliciano sang the most heartfelt version, and while Elston Howard's daughter's interpretation was remarkable, it was also the s-l-o-w-e-s-t. I love my country and Robert Merrill's take on the anthem as much as the next guy, but I was at the game to make a dollar, so I tried to keep moving or else I lost money. When teams come in from Canada, that country's anthem is also played, so it is doubly important to keep track of the time properly. For a vendor, it's very true—time *is* money. I always stopped for the man or woman in uniform out of respect, but if a runner-up from *America's Got Talent* was doing the anthem, I hustled into the station as fast as I could.

Another way to save some time is to go back to the station before having finished selling out. Let's say my item is soda and I am near the section where the station is located, but I still have three soda bottles left in my tray. Rather than continuing to walk around, trying to sell those last three sodas, since I was near the station, I replenished and continued on my way. Though I did have a heavier load by having three sodas in addition to the twenty-four in the new case, in the long run, I was using my time better. Just know your limit; eight extra sodas might be too much.

They would set up a microphone down there for the anthem

Avoid hazards. The hot dog vendors, in their haste, often drop the small single-serving packets of ketchup and mustard onto the ground, leaving a perilous trail. I tried to be careful not to step on this minefield, which can be tricky, since I often couldn't look down to see where I was going, as my tray or case was in the way. The advice I got from an old-time vendor in one of my early years was, "Slide the foot and sweep. You don't need to *see* 'em. You can *feel* 'em."

It's also important to be wary of fans, usually kids,

intentionally stomping on these packets for their own amusement. These little grenades squoosh and can completely splatter uniforms. Once that happens, there's a big blotch of yellow or red on the pants leg. Oftentimes, I was not even aware of it until I got down to the locker room at the end of the game. The last time it happened to me, I had a big splotch of ketchup all over my pants leg along the shin. One of the vendors saw it and said to me, "Takin' one for the team, huh, Stew?"

Sometimes, I might be walking through a corridor and someone stops short... and my item went flying out of my hands. In that instance, I'd gather my product quietly, without an argument, and carry on. It can happen a lot, but I suggest taking the high road. Letting off steam is just not worth it. Trust me... If you want to last forty years, that is.

When walking down a tight aisle, I always kept my elbows tucked in, to nuzzle my way through. On the other hand, when I wanted to avoid a mob in a corridor, I spread my elbows wide like an eagle expanding its wings, to give me more room. When trying to negotiate a busy area, one veteran beer vendor called out "Hot Stuff," which always worked to part the throng. Ya gotta do what ya gotta do!

It's important to keep your apron tied snug around you. Once in a while, I have felt it drooping on me, and when that happened, I could feel my coins banging and clanging up against my knee. In those instances, it's best to stop what you are doing, retie the apron, and get on with it.

Before a game started, many of the seats would be placed down. If I was not looking where I was going, I often smacked my shin into them. Not a good feeling. Self-inflicted black-and-blue marks from low-slung aprons or poorly hinged seats are bad. I have had welts last up to three homestands simply because I was in too much of a rush to either watch where I was going or stop and retie.

If selling peanuts or Cracker Jack, it's fun to toss the bag to the customer—it's an intrinsic part of being a vendor and getting the fans involved. However, it's not a good idea to toss a twenty-ounce plastic water bottle across a row. I've seen rookie vendors attempt it, and when it hits someone, it's not good, not fun, and not *intrinsic*. Avoid bottle tossing at all times.

Be patient. I have worked on some absolutely dreadful days when I couldn't sell beer even if it was half price. Those games, I would call out, "Hey beer here!" and it echoed as if I were yelling into the Grand Canyon. Sometimes, my patience got stretched, and I often called out to unresponsive crowds,
"Hey, is this mike on?"
"Are you a painting or what?"
"I know you're out there... I hear you breathing."
"Anyone...? Anyone... Bueller??"
Vendor life can be especially tough when an item is not selling, whether it's a holiday weekend, a brutally cold or hot day, or simply bad luck. Keep going. During many games, I have wanted to quit after each case, but plowing on, I would eventually make a day's pay. That's the trick: just as in life—keep going. Perhaps you've walked around your sections for what seems like forever and you've given fans directions to their seats or to the nearest bathroom and the closest you've come to making a sale is a little kid coming up and asking, "How much?" Not *if*, but when this happens to you, all I can say is, be patient.

The weather can be nasty at times, and I often found myself sloshing through rain delays. Every day doesn't suck; only some of them. There was one rain delay where the fans waited over *three hours* for the game to start. That night, I was the only beer vendor who didn't quit early and was told I could stay through the delay if I wanted to, but once the game started, I had to go home. Only true diehards hang in for such long rain delays, and these fans may want a beer simply because the tarp finally came off the field. So, after the final words of the national anthem were sung at 10:30, I immediately followed, "...and the home... of the ... brave" with, "Last Call!" I almost got shot.

Expect the unexpected. It's hard to predict consistently how business will be, so Friday nights are not necessarily better than Tuesday nights. And, contrary to belief, it is actually much easier to sell twelve cases of beer than it is to sell five. Why? When I sold five cases, I walked through the stands longer and had to lug a fuller case for a greater period of time. When business was not good, I would hike up to the back row for a sale, whereas when business was brisk, I might never get all the way up there, cut off by thirsty customers along the way. If I was selling quickly, my case was always getting lighter and the work time went faster, as the rhythm and the energy of the crowd helped keep me moving. Strange as it may sound, it's always easier to sell *more* than *less*.

Whenever I had a scorecard gate and found myself chatting with people to my right, I kept my hand on my stack of programs to my left, so I could *feel* them. This was important, as sometimes those programs had the ability to walk away or, more specifically, were taken away. I usually trust my fellow man, but not my fellow fan. The same was true with my beer case. If it was on the ground as I was servicing a customer, I kept my foot on it or against it, so I could feel or sense if someone was sticking their mitts in there. I'm not saying pilfering happens *all* the time; I'm just sayin' it happens.

Be sure to check the ID from the fans as thoroughly as possible. I often asked kids what their zip code was when they didn't resemble the picture on their driver's license. Once I did this, they often looked like the proverbial deer in the headlights. Phony IDs are very easy to acquire, so check and double check. The job you save may be your own.

Be careful not to make assumptions. For instance, on any particular night, after starting to sell at 7 o'clock, I might look up at the scoreboard and see it was 8 and realize I had sold four cases of beer. If I had another hour and a half of selling, I might have thought I was on course to sell six more cases, for a total of ten for the game. But assuming that may prove frustrating. I have often sold four in an hour and then only one more in the next hour and a half because, very often, sales die. D—I—E.

Assume nothing. On some days, the numbers start early, and on others, the second half of the night is where the money is. Just keep going and add it all up at the end of the night. Again. Trust me.

Sometimes it's best to just walk away. I can attest to this one wholeheartedly. On many occasions, as I would finish up my case, I might have only one beer left in my bin. Often, a fan may put up two fingers, indicating they wanted two beers. The conversation usually went something like this:

"I only have one left."
"I need two."
"*Uh*... I only have one."
"But I need two."
"You want the one?"
"I need two."

This is the point where the thought comes to me...*sometimes it's best to just walk away*. The customer is always right, especially when they're wrong, but sometimes, just as in life, that's a crock of you-know-what.

BRONX SCIENCE

THE BRONX IS KNOWN worldwide for the Yankees and their stadium, of course, but also for the largest zoo in America and the Bronx High School of Science. Often referred to as "Bronx Science," it is highly ranked internationally and home to numerous Pulitzer and Nobel Prize winners. I didn't go there—admissions required something they referred to as "good grades"—but my personal travels gave me my education, my own version of "Bronx Science."

Watch the vendors at a game sometime. A good one works extremely hard and is particularly courteous to the customers because he or she knows their paycheck depends on it. Oh, how I wish that were true in the "real world." If a postal clerk were paid a commission on how many customers they handled in a day, then we wouldn't have to wait on line so long. Same with supermarket cashiers or virtually anyone who gets paid hourly or any worker who needs a jolt to do their job a little quicker and a little more effectively. I know working on commission can cause certain competitive problems within a company, but I have a feeling, if I were paid by the hour, I'd spend more time looking at a clock than looking at a customer. I guess that's why I never had a steady 9-to-5 gig.

Vendors hustle because, if they don't, they go home empty-handed. Even when selling ice cream on a sub-freezing cold day or licorice in the upper deck or some other lousy item, it's important to hang in there. The weekly check doesn't know what was earned from one day to the next, but it all adds up in the end.

I can recall selling hot chocolate in the old stadium when the sun would come out and the temperature suddenly went up twenty degrees. Yet it was important to finish that day's job, make whatever I could, and perhaps the next game I would get a better item. I've worked when the soda was flat, the dogs were cold, and the popcorn was stale. I've had sections of visiting Mormons from Utah when I was selling beer and nobody would buy a single one.

I've been assigned beer on camp-themed afternoon games when the only person in a section who *could* buy was the team's coach, and he was chaperoning the kids, so he *couldn't* buy, even though he probably needed one. Or on sloppy, sloshy, wet nights, when the rain delay dragged on and on. I have been assigned ice cream cups on days when the porters forgot to pick up spoons for me from downstairs and I never left the station. During those rough stretches, I would often come home and tell my dad how poorly I did, yet he encouraged me to hang in there. On those days when sales were weak, my vending buddy, Keith, often quoted his grandfather, who said, "Oatmeal's better than no meal."

I have also come to realize that, in my acting world, if I don't hustle, if I don't seek out an audition, contact my agent on some casting news I've found out about, or even get a new agent if they don't hold up their end of our business relationship, I *will* go home empty-handed. And sometimes I may be rehearsing for weeks, performing in a play for very little or even no money, and then make out pretty well on a commercial for working one single day.

The stadium taught me a lot about myself. I tend to get jealous of people. Jealous of other vendors who had better items than I did, jealous of fans who had pretty girlfriends while I was stuck in the bleachers, and jealous of people who were at a barbeque on Memorial Day while I was struggling to sell peanuts to a half-empty ballpark as the Yanks played the White Sox. Over time, I managed to stay somewhat sane by reminding myself, "Tomorrow, I will get the better item to sell. Tomorrow, I will be with my girlfriend, having fun somewhere. And tomorrow, when everyone is back at their jobs after their holiday weekend, I'll be off from work and free to go wherever I please."

Experience makes one realize there will be another day, until eventually there isn't.

Over the years, I have been smacked in the head by handfuls of peanuts, half-eaten hot dogs, crunched-up balls of wet, soiled napkins, ice cubes, partially filled plastic bottles, and basically anything the fans deemed throw-able. My first few years, I admit, I mouthed off at times, but I did learn how to duck and think quickly on my feet, in order to keep my job. Fans need to let off a little steam, and the ballpark is the perfect place for them to do it. They spent a lot of money on their tickets, so if fans got their frustrations out by treating me rudely, I did my best to try to understand why, though certain nights it may have been difficult.

And sometimes, when a batter got a broken-bat single in the bottom of the seventh for the Yanks to take the lead, I would see off-duty mailmen, often still in their uniforms, having hustled to the game straight from work, "high-fiving" perfect strangers. People everywhere, *from* everywhere, are looking for that little base hit with a runner on second to help them get through their day.

After a game, I might hear a vendor in the locker room complain that he sold ten beers to a group of fans and didn't get a "subway" or tip for his trouble. "Man, ten friggin' beers and they didn't give me nothing."

Sometimes that vendor was, in fact, *me,* but over the years I grew to realize, "You sold them $80 worth of beer, and at your commission rate, you made pretty good money in less than a minute. That's nothing to complain about." If the expectations are lower, the chance of being disappointed is lower, as well.

While I was in acting school, I performed in the play, *The Diary of Anne Frank*. My role was "Mr. Dussel," a middle-aged dentist in Amsterdam during World War II, who shared a room in the attic with the teenaged Anne.

Looks like a rough night

As part of my characterization, I chose to give him a limp. I was only twenty-three at the time, and I felt it would not only age him but also humanize him, as he was a very cold person to Anne and the others in hiding. I also gave "Mr. Dussel" a Dutch accent as part of my portrayal. In Anne Frank's world, everyone spoke Dutch, not English, so an accent was not only unrealistic but also unnecessary. For the flavor of the play, however, I chose to add this dialect to complement my characterization.

Following the production, which, at the American Academy of Dramatic Arts was only one performance, I went to speak to the president and vice-president of the school, to get an assessment of my work. This was standard practice, as a frank discussion with these decision-makers was necessary for me to grow and learn my craft. What they told me was a lesson that has stayed with me my entire life.

One of these men was complimentary about my limp, telling

me how realistic and effective it was in giving "Mr. Dussel" the humanity I was seeking. But when I went down the hall to speak to the other administrator, he told me how much he *hated* the limp, how distracting it was, and that I had "bit off more than I could chew." By having a limp and an accent in a somewhat simple, modified school production, I had clearly overreached. With a short rehearsal period, he reasoned, I hadn't had substantial time to hone these attributes, and I should have simply stuck to the emotional life of my character for the performance.

Being twenty-three and a neophyte-acting student, I was obviously impressionable and confused. Back then, I had large dreams for my career. I even imagined myself directing a film version of *Of Mice and Men* where I played all the male parts, including the old black farmhand, "Crooks." My only concern was I wasn't sure if I could pull off the part of "Curly's Wife." I've got nice legs, but....

In regards to *Anne Frank*, which administrator was my young ego to believe—the one who had praised me or the one who had criticized me for overreaching? It was here that I took my mother's longstanding advice: "Listen to what people have to say, then do what you want anyway." From that point on, I realized that two opposing ideas can still be true or both can even be false, but *I* must trust my gut. So, though patience is a virtue, he who hesitates is lost. Both are clichés and both are often true. Circumstances can make one expression truer than the other. Trust your gut, always—as an actor, as a vendor, as a man.

New Yorkers can be tough, as we know, and when I saw a fan wearing a Cleveland Indians hat or a Detroit Tigers T-shirt, I usually felt empathy for them. I knew they were going to be in for some ridicule from the partisan Yankee fans that day—it was inevitable. Out in the stands, I witnessed some brutal behavior from the locals as they often verbally and, sometimes, *physically* abused fans who were rooting for the visiting team.

Occasionally, fistfights broke out, especially at the old stadium, where security guards were in short supply. I thought, "That poor Orioles fan is in for it. It's going to be tough for him to get through nine innings of heckling—or worse."

The fans visiting from out of town got me thinking on a larger scale. I had customers who were from all over the world, whether I was conducting business at my souvenir booth or vending in the stands. More importantly, I worked alongside fellow New Yorkers who also may have been Haitians, Columbians, Cubans, Asians, South Africans, Rastafarians, and many others who looked and sounded much differently than I did. By growing up and summering in the Bronx, taking acting classes, working in the city, driving shotgun with my dad in Harlem, and learning from my mom's freewheelin' attitude with so many people, I grew to believe:

> *We are **all** members of a minority...*
> *Just depends where you're standing.*

If a white male is in a Kenyan village, there's a strong chance he's a minority there. A Hindu woman in a church—minority. Irish Catholic in a mosque—minority. The same goes for a Korean in Oklahoma or a black person in Sweden. And, for that matter, even the poor Orioles fan in the Bronx. Minority. But if the Hindu woman is placed in New Delhi, the Korean in Seoul, *and* even that lonely Orioles fan in Baltimore, then it's a completely different story. Seems simple, but I think we often forget the simple when it comes to how we treat each other.

When I was vending, I would often sell to a cultural cross section of a hundred customers a day. At my souvenir stand, I was able to converse with people, and I got to recognize and appreciate our similarities. The grandmother from Wisconsin and the tourists from Japan were a lot like me, even though we grew up in different cultures with dissimilar backgrounds. Small talk and the love of baseball brought us together.

Like anyone who is Jewish, I have dealt with anti-Semitism

from time to time. When I was in acting school in Manhattan, I was one of only two Jews in my class, and I was often mistaken for Allan Katz, and he for me. We were clumped together, often in derogatory ways.

"Stew-The-Jew" is what I was often called when I would run out to hustle my last case of beer towards the end of a game, when there was only five minutes left before management cut off sales. Sometimes, I overheard "Stew-The-Jew" from the checker, the banker, the porters, other vendors, and sometimes I didn't know where it came from, but I definitely heard it.

When I had my souvenir stand and I replenished my stock, remarks came from the guys who worked down in the room, who were mostly Italian and Irish, often much younger than I was. They were too immature or unaware to realize that Italians, Irish, or anyone who happens to be in the wrong neighborhood are also minorities, just like the rest of us. Being in the minority at the stadium often bothered me, no question, but I gradually understood that disparaging comments often come out of ignorance and insecurity.

An ex-girlfriend of mine once took me to an office party. She was excited to introduce me to her co-workers and especially to her boss. It was a large event being held at a catering hall, so it was a big deal. We were a little late, and once we got there, we headed over to her boss's table, where he was holding court in front of a dozen of his employees.

Just as we made it to the table, he was finishing up a joke, and we were able to hear him roar out the punch line, "...so what do I look like—a *JEW*?"

I took a deep breath as the table erupted with laughter. I'm not sure if it was because the joke was funny or if they were being polite to their employer, but at that function, *this* Jew was in the minority, no doubt about it.

When I visited another ex during one particular Christmas vacation, I hadn't known her for very long at the time, and her family didn't really know me. They were Massachusetts religious WASPs, and the head of the table was a bit of a blowhard who thought the world owed him something.

He was head of security at a prominent university in Worcester, and a dozen people sat around the table, with me again as the outsider, as the conversation went from this to that. One tale included a story about someone named "Schwartz." That someone happened to be me—my real last name, which I had changed to "Zully" for the sake of show business.

Zully had been my father's first name; Sigmund, in Hungarian. Early in my acting career, I thought I'd be able to get a wider array of parts if I had a last name that had a vague origin. "Is he Greek? Is he Italian? We don't know, but let's cast him." Or so I thought. And I know it worked for me at least one time, when I was cast on *Law and Order* as an ex-church choirboy. I'm not sure they would have even let me audition if my name had still been Schwartz.

So, Zully became my stage name, but my driver's license was mismarked, listing my name as "Schwartzakazully." By not placing spaces around "aka," the Motor Vehicle Bureau caused me to get stopped at airport security every flight I took. Eventually, I changed it legally and said goodbye to the name Schwartz, along with the hassles at La Guardia.

Anyway, when the conversation came to my name at my ex's Christmas dinner in Worcester, this big bully of a father of hers chimed in. "How do you spell Schwartz? *J-E-W?*"

The table went "Yuk, yuk, yuk," heartily laughing with Dad, while I, however, silently went, *Yeccch!* Uh, *check* please!

As individuals, we obviously have a lot in common, no matter what our last name might be. We have all been nervous the first day of school or at a new job, feeling alone and outside the larger group, managing to make us a minority, which, under those circumstances, we are. But, after all, we're humans first, with essentially similar needs and desires.

Everyone, in my estimation, no matter who they are, wants to feed and clothe their family, have a roof over their heads, live freely with a sense of dignity, and, as my mother used to say, "do good."

"Life, liberty, and the pursuit of happiness" may have been written for Americans, but shouldn't it apply to everyone, everywhere, whatever ethnicity, whatever color, and whatever religion?

Is it trite to say we should attempt to understand each other and have more patience with someone who might not look quite like us or who worships in a different place than we do? Whenever I started a new role in the theater, I had to go back to square one to do my work, go back to the basics of who my character was, what he wanted from the other people in the play, etc. When acting, you can't skip these crucial steps; you must always go back to the beginning, to get on the right track. I am trying to do the same when I first meet people: go back to the beginning, to see them with the same desires and needs as anyone else.

Some of my fellow vendors and co-workers at the ballpark came from large black families in the Carolinas or broken homes in San Juan. Some were Chinese immigrants and others were Slavic from Connecticut. But we all came together to earn a living. We got dressed together in the locker room as a diverse group, yet with a common goal as vendors.

My Bronx Science and street sense taught me that most valuable of lessons:

> We are **all** members of a minority...
> Just depends where you're standing.

THE FINAL SEASON: YOGI, IT'S OVER

NEVER IN MY WILDEST dreams, in all my years as a vendor, did I think I would outlive the old Yankee Stadium. My dad worked there for five years in the thirties, my uncle worked for a year or two as well, a few of my nephews tried it for a couple of games, and it's been an essential part of my entire adult life.

The old stadium is where I grew up and spent my summers. I worked out of every station—the bleachers, the lower deck, the loge, and the uppers. I sold ice cream, dogs, cotton candy, hot chocolate, beer, wine coolers, soda, pretzels, pizza rolls, peanuts, and M&M's. I manned a souvenir stand at every location available to me, including the extremely prime real estate in the hallway corridor behind home plate, where the high-priced customers shopped. I worked in snow and sleet, rain and fog, hundred-degree scorchers and below-freezing football games. And I also sat in seats from all angles at games I attended as a fan and at those games after I'd finished working. The old joint was my home, and, I must admit, seeing it slip away slowly tore at my guts. For over 2500 events, I hung out with the guys until call time, dealt with thousands and thousands of fans, and eked out a living or, more correctly, part of a living.

The final year, 2008, was going to be like no other. Tickets were swept up extremely early, and all weekend games were sold out by mid-February, nearly two months before the season even began. Joe Torre, their hugely successful manager for twelve years, decided to leave and went to the rival Los Angeles Dodgers during the winter. Things around the Bronx were certainly going to be different, that's for sure.

Opening day usually occurs during the month of April, but in 2008, for the first time, it was scheduled for March 31. Perhaps the unusual date was a sign of a unique year to come, as it rained all day and, after a long wait, the game was postponed to the next day. For over eighty years the Yankees home openers were always in April, and the rainout kept that streak alive.

On opening days, we found out which fellow vendors or counter workers passed away during the off-season, what the latest handshakes were coming out of the "hood" (interlocking fingers, snaps, high, low, etc.), and whether or not our waist had gone up or down by the size pants we picked up from the linen room. The opener had the added element that it would be the last in the old ballpark, so it was rather odd, as we got ready in the locker room, to climb those stairs for the start of the final season.

In addition, there were rumors circulating that our employers were getting dumped, and *we* might not be coming back to the stadium, either. During every homestand of the final season, we heard speculation that our livelihoods were on the line. And if we were going to get rehired, would we be able to keep our seniority? Who were going to be our new bosses? The final season started for me with legitimate uncertainty about my job, and I remained in doubt throughout the entire year.

Before each home game, the fans would line up early at Gate 2, the closest entrance in from the subway. They then would respectfully stroll through Monument Park and have their photos taken next to the monuments that represented heroes to Yankee fans from everywhere. Many of these Hall of Famers epitomized the Yankee tradition, giants who spanned generations of greatness.

During this final season, more and more people brought cameras in than in the past. Throughout the year, I was constantly bumping into fans taking pictures, especially when Derek Jeter or Alex Rodriguez came up to the plate. These fans would huddle in the main aisle that snaked through the lower deck and beg the ushers, who were supposed to keep the area clear, to let them flash, shoot, and click away. For the vendors, it was a nuisance, since we were still hustling to sell our beer and these people were often in our way. The ballpark's mystique had worn off for me years earlier, but when I finally brought in *my* camera, I understood what all the commotion was about.

Monument Park

I recall coming in early one game and taking a picture of the brilliant façade. The memory of when I had been a fan in the sixties, before becoming a vendor, came rushing back to me. Bleacher seats were seventy-five cents back then, but I usually sat in the grandstand, under that same façade in the upper deck, for a dollar fifty. Reserved seats were two-fifty, and the best seats in the house were three-fifty box seats. I tried to sneak down there if I could for the last out, like I used to do with my mother at the Knicks basketball games, but I also remember one day seeing a ticket on the ground when I was about eleven. It was a box seat ticket, and it got me so nervous, I was afraid to even pick it up. It completely spooked me. Wow! A box seat ticket at Yankee Stadium—that's for Elvis Presley or Jackie O or somebody like that.

All-Star week took place in mid-July. In order to secure a scorecard gate for those days, I had to show up an hour before the turnstiles opened so, as per my seniority, I could man a key spot where the fans would pass through while entering. I often got what's called a backup gate, not a prime gate, which is reserved for vendors with higher seniority than me. In the final season, there were fourteen vendors who had been at the ballpark longer than I had, and most of them chose the more lucrative locations than I was able to rate.

There were a number of events spread over the days of All-Star week that initially were cause for excitement. Unfortunately, the first was something called "A Futures Game," featuring young, promising players, followed by a celebrity softball game. Seeing celebs and soap opera stars play on the field might have been fun for the fans, but it wasn't any help for business. I sold three boxes of scorecards at my backup gate, cashed out, and then sold a few cases of beer. The day was, frankly, a disappointment—an overhyped yawn.

The next night was the home-run derby, when Josh Hamilton of the Texas Rangers hit twenty-eight homers in one round, a derby record. They were towering shots—three of them supposedly went over 500 feet, yet I didn't see a single one of them because I was running around, setting up a scorecard booth for the "blow-off." On derby night, I hadn't rated a gate at all for the start of the game, not even a backup, so this was a consolation.

Whenever a game ended and the fans were exiting the ballpark, that exiting was known as "the blow-off." Those vendors who have a souvenir stand anxiously wait for this time, as fans often hold off until the game is over to pick up an item for themselves or their kids at home. Whenever something historic happens at a game, whether it be a no-hitter, a 500th career home run, a 3000th career hit, big strikeout games for a pitcher, etc., it's important to set up for the "blow-off" to have as profitable a workday as possible.

There have been games when I was vending hot dogs or beer, and I'd realized there was a no-hitter going on and, with that possibility, the blow-off had an extra twist to it. If it was the eighth inning and there seemed to be a chance of a no-hitter, instead of going home after checking out in the seventh inning, I would go to the souvenir room to see if I could get a few boxes of scorecards. Fans who have attended a no-hitter, whether *for* the Yankees or *against* them, like to have a souvenir program as a keepsake; I tried to take advantage of making the extra money whenever I could.

The trick is, once I had signed out for two or three boxes of programs, I needed to find an exit gate that hadn't already been secured by another quick-thinking vendor. Sometimes, I would find a good spot, but another vendor might come along moments later and set up right in front of me, usually around a wall and down a corridor, so I couldn't see him.

This practice was dirty and against a code of ethics for vendors. However, it was done just the same, and I often had to negotiate my position with the vendor who was attempting to "piggyback" on my gate. Then I would wait out the game, hoping the pitcher hung in there to complete the no-hitter.

I often found myself with a beautiful spot, at the ready with my boxes, only to have someone get a hit in the ninth inning and mess up the whole plan. Then I had to bring all of the boxes back to the souvenir room to get credit for them, accompanied by groans from the crew in there for having to do the extra work of taking the returns.

That's baseball. With apologies to Yogi, "It ain't a no-hitter until it's a no-hitter." But over my tenure, I was rewarded with no-hitters thrown by Jim Abbott, David Cone, Dwight Gooden, Dave Righetti, and David Wells.

When setting up, it's important, as you open the first box of programs, to break down the carton so you are able to stand on the broken-down box. A little cushion like that helps the strain on the feet over a long period of time. Cashiers in grocery stores are usually standing on some sort of mat or cardboard box. Easier on the feet.

On the night of the home-run derby, I went to gate 6, which was the exit nearest the right field foul pole. On one of these memorable, special nights—and Hamilton's record-setting home runs on derby night qualified—I usually tried to increase sales by calling out: "*Historic Program Here! Get Your Program!*"

The day itself was called "The Gatorade All-Star Workout Day," so I didn't feel guilty about trumping up my product—they trumped up theirs. In fact, they wanted us employees to wear a pin of some kind during All-Star Week, but I don't like to do that unless I get paid a little extra. I get compensated for commercials when using my name and likeness, so I don't like to give myself away, not even my chest.

But never mind that, this program *was* a historic program. And I always enjoyed seeing someone walk past me during those moments as they were exiting and then suddenly hear my call, reach their hand into their pocket, and come back and ask me for a program. It's a mystery how many fans I sold to over the years—tourists, locals, whomever—as they danced out of the ballpark on one of those memorable days.

The All-Star game itself went into extra innings... a *lot* of extra innings. In a long, slow game that goes late, the employees go from grumpy to angry to delirious to running on empty to flat-out loopy.

After a few extra innings, the vendors and security personnel endured numerous moments, sensing the end was near, but by the time I was on the 4 train platform heading home, it was 2:30 in the morning. I had started the day at 3 that afternoon, so the final season's All-Star game was quite a bit longer than a usual day at the ballpark for me. The money was good, but the fatigue was not.

The final old-timer's game, which was a gathering of more

than seventy former Yankees, consisted of a mix of players from little-known Mickey Klutts to Hall-of-Famer Reggie Jackson. Throughout the years, I always had a soft spot for the old-timer's games, a Saturday afternoon, usually in July, though for the final year it was in August to accommodate the elongated All-Star week. I worked old-timer's games when Mantle, Rizzuto, Berra, and DiMaggio stood along the first base line during introductions with the likes of Billy Martin, Whitey Ford, Roy White, Hank Bauer, Moose Skowron, and Joe Pepitone. Those days were always fun, seeing the heroes of my youth carrying around more weight than they had during their playing years... but far less hair.

Number 7— Mickey Mantle

The old stadium's final season was not a good one for the Yanks, since they failed to make the playoffs after having successfully done so for thirteen straight years. Usually, scouts from pennant-contending teams could be seen observing the Yankees in anticipation of meeting them in that year's playoffs. These men, who in years past smoked cheap, stinky cigars at their seats behind home plate, would be armed with speed guns for tracking the pitcher's fastball. They would spread reports and clipboards on their laps and adjoining seats, taking notes on situational baseball and trying to get a strategic edge for their team. In past seasons, whenever I was vending behind the plate and saw them, my love for statistics tempted me to drop everything and shoot the shit, talking about one player's weakness for the change-up or another's speed going from first to third on a single to right. But, in this final year, the scouts were starting to dwindle by early September, a sure sign that the Yanks weren't going to be playing post-season baseball.

All through the year, tension built as giant numbers on the scoreboard counted down to the final game. Sometime around mid-August, with twenty games left, I started to recognize the end was *really* coming. The fans, however, sensed it sooner and started pilfering signs and memorabilia throughout the year. One night, I saw a fan leave with a toilet seat he'd somehow dislodged from a men's room. I wonder, though, how does he prove authenticity if he tries to sell it on EBay? I guess that's his problem.

The very last weeks carried with them a feeling of dread. The stock market was sinking miserably, the Mets were going through a horrible tank job for the second straight year, and pessimism was rampant throughout the city. In addition, we vendors still hadn't received final word on our future and ultimately didn't find out until the winter months of the off-season whether we'd be moving across the street with the team. As it turned out, our employers got bought out and were not coming with us, but the new concessions company ensured that I, at least, still had my job to look forward to.

The final day game in Yankee Stadium took place on Saturday afternoon, September 20, 2008. Fortunately, it was a glorious day, temperature around seventy degrees under sunny skies, and I got to meet the documentary filmmaker Ken Burns in the stands, sitting behind the Yankee dugout. I offered Burns a beer and told him that I loved the fifth-inning installment of his baseball documentary, which was absolutely brilliant filmmaking about our national pastime. He passed on the beer but perked up and mentioned the episode by name, "Shadow Ball," which covered the era of the Negro Leagues. I was able to tell him of my admiration for his work on the Civil War and jazz documentaries, as well as those on baseball. Chatting up Burns, one of our country's greatest historians, the day before the stadium closed its doors was apropos for the occasion.

The Yankee organization knows how to throw a party, and the final night was no exception. The game, a nationally televised celebration, was one of the hottest tickets in New York sports history, with people spending thousands of dollars to pay their final respects. All fans who arrived early were allowed to stroll around the warning track and touch the foul pole and the outfield wall. The team arranged for great stars from the past to gather at the bases and at every fielding position in an elaborate ceremony prior to the opening pitch.

There was a sacred mood in the air—not unlike when the Pope makes his occasional visits to the Bronx. The thing was, on this closing night, there was no Pope. Yet there was a tremendous amount of love pouring out from the fans to their baseball heroes—the greatest ovations going to Paul O'Neill, Scott Brosius, Phil Rizzuto's wife Clara, Mickey Mantle's son David, and perhaps the loudest ovation of all to their recent star, Bernie Williams.

It was truly baseball heaven that night, complete with the Babe's ninety-two-year-old daughter throwing out the first pitch. So many fans were reminded of their previous visits to the ballpark, climbing the ramps to the upper deck or sneaking downstairs as a kid or bringing a glove for batting practice or waiting for an autograph with dad or keeping score for the first time. Yet the elephant in the stadium was a feeling not unlike visiting a loved one in a hospital whom you knew you wouldn't be seeing again. It was a celebration of an historical landmark, but it was oddly strange at the same time. The fans seemed to refuse to say goodbye, not wanting the night to end. Everyone who was there will never forget it, that's for sure.

One vendor later told me a curious story about that night. He had a customer complain about spending $34 for four beers. Granted, a lot of money, but the vendor asked the fan, "How much did you pay for your tickets on Stubhub?"

"$1000 each," the fan replied.

The vendor then said, "So you're complaining about being charged eight-fifty for a fucking beer—you gotta be kiddin' me?" Blunt talk, no doubt, from a vendor to a fan, but the customer felt so shamed, he told the vendor to keep the two twenties he paid him with and then gave him another fifty on top of it—a $56 tip for four beers!

Around the seventh inning of the final night, I made my way over to say goodbye to a fan who had been one of my regulars for many years. He had season tickets in the left field box seats, and he often sat with his headphones on and always stayed to the end of the games, whether his team won or lost, and no matter if it was cold or hot, wet or dry. He was primarily a Coors drinker, so I decided to give him my Coors price badge as a souvenir.

When I did, he gave me a huge bear hug that shook me to the core. He did everything he could from breaking down in tears right in my arms, and I felt the exact same way. We stepped back, looked at each other, and said, "Have a great winter See ya next year." We'd said that at the end of every season, but, of course, this time the words had a different feeling. This time, they had a hollow sensation to them, that elephant-in-the-stadium kind of hollow. It was tough. Real tough.

I myself didn't want to stick around to the very end of the game, so I missed Derek Jeter taking the microphone and addressing the crowd with his heartfelt speech. I also didn't get to see the team running around the edge of the lower level, waving and shaking hands with their fans. So much of my life has been tied to that place, nearly forty summers spent in the Bronx, so it was just too difficult for me to stay. Weeks later, I read a quote from the great sportswriter Roger Angell regarding the final game played by the New York Giants in the Polo Grounds fifty-odd years earlier. It seemed to apply to Yankee Stadium's final night as well.

I didn't feel anything. Nothing at all. I guess I just couldn't believe it. But it's true, all right. The flags are down, the lights in the temple are out, and The Harlem River flows lonely to the sea.

I managed to get to the vendor locker room early before most of the guys got down. Usually, a final game is filled with mixed emotion—fatigue from a long year coming to an end, and good wishes for co-workers to have a safe winter. This time, though, we had to say goodbye to the building, as well. The Yankees went on to beat the Orioles on this final night, 7-3, so at least they went out with a win. I got downstairs and shook a few hands and saw my boss, who had been gracious and affable and started her Yankee career after I'd been a vendor for about ten years. I told her I had been working in this building for thirty-seven years, and she looked at me and sarcastically joked, "That's your problem." But on this particular night, the *true* problem for me was that I was sure to have a knot in my stomach for quite some time.

In the old stadium, there was a sense of camaraderie between the workers and our employers, the concessions company. For instance, I used to be able to go to the ticket booth before a game, and, as a vendor, I was given a little priority. It was courteous of them, as it showed appreciation for my being part of the family. In the new stadium, the Yankee organization took over the vending duties in a shared partnership with the

Dallas Cowboys and Goldman Sachs; the corporate relationship with our bosses took some getting used to, as it was much more formal. Nevertheless, the vendors have helped make the new conglomerate's transition a relatively easy one.

During the last game, one vendor, a real tough guy with tattoos on his tattoos including a Yankee logo on one of his forearms, was totally devastated. I will never forget seeing him rest his tray on a railing, crying like a five-year-old. I had to pat him on the back and console him just as so many had to console so many others that night.

When it was time for me to go, I walked to the subway with a strong pace, never looking back at the ballpark. I was determined to get to the platform without giving in to one more peek. I'd seen it for forty years—did I really need to see it again?

Even Yogi Berra, the ultimate character and quite possibly the most beloved of all Yankees (admit it: nobody don't like Yogi), was disconsolate. I later heard he nearly broke down at a news conference when he was reminded of former teammates who had all passed on. He spoke for so many when he said of the closing of the stadium, "It will always be in my heart. I'm sorry to see it over, I tell you that."

Me, too, Yogi. Me, too.

NEW STADIUM, NEW ERA

I'M OLD SCHOOL, what can I say? I think it takes more to "like" someone than simply being instructed to do so on Facebook. And what do they mean "friend" me? I've spent a lifetime finding, nurturing, and keeping my friends, and clicking a button had nothing to do with it. And I never was much for watching a television show and voting for an "idol." Puh-lease.

When I walk into a drugstore for my toothpaste, I see all kinds of flavors for Crest. I can get citrus, cool winter green, bubble gum, mint, herbal mint, clean mint, mint gel, cool peppermint liquid gel, minty fresh striped—everything but original paste. I don't want "New and Improved." I want "Old and Lousy." If I could find some Crest original paste, I would buy a whole case of the stuff so I could go to sleep knowing I can have my flavor. Sometimes I feel as if I'm being tortured.

"Hey, Crest! No one would have ever heard of you if it weren't for the first one. What happened to original paste?"

I mention all of this because Yankee Stadium as I've known it is gone, and the "new and improved" model has now taken its place. Many have said and written that the only reason the old ballpark was leveled was because there weren't enough high-priced luxury boxes, elite seating, and exclusive bars and restaurants for the Fortune 500 companies to be able to pamper their clients. My "old and lousy" stadium actually had more overall seats than the new one, but it only had a certain amount of luxury boxes, so a completely new ballpark was built to satisfy this need. I mean greed. I mean need.

Yankee Stadium has always stood right next to two subway stops in the Bronx, and one of the old ballpark's great virtues was that it was truly for the people of New York, its working class citizens. It also catered to tourists, of course, but since the new stadium cost one and a half billion dollars, we can say goodbye to the working-class fans and hello to thousand-dollar seats, ten-dollar hot dogs, and a twenty-dollar scorecard. That's progress, I guess.

Years ago, the Yankees used to give away items to lure fans into the ballpark. Bat Day was the first, which led to Cap Day, Helmet Day, Ball Day, and on and on. Now, of course, there is everything from Magnet Schedule Day to Mousepad Night.

The team does not need these giveaways to lure crowds anymore, since every year since 1996 they have averaged over 40,000 fans per game. Now the companies use the freebies to hawk their products.

> *Welcome to Nestle's Wristband Night! The Yankees wish to thank Verizon for sponsoring Batting Glove Day. Let's all give the CEO a warm round of applause.*

Baseball used to be a sport, but now, of course, it's a business—a *huge* business. Players take steroids to have better statistics, get an enormous multi-year contract, and then, years later, admit to it with little, if any, penalty for their transgressions. The age of innocence, which perhaps was simply in my naive mind, is over. Players used to love the game. Now, they love the money.

In one of the final years of the old stadium, the Yanks had another corporate-sponsored giveaway night. As I was walking through the stands before the game started, selling my beer, I glanced down at the field, and there were a few oversized mascots near home plate. Then I heard the deep, stentorian tones of public address announcer Bob Sheppard finishing a sentence,

"And the Yankees...value...their relationship...with Pokemon."

That shook me, it really did. I breathed a moment and then I silently thanked God for taking Babe Ruth before he'd had a chance to show up at an event dressed as SpongeBob SquarePants. Progress? I wonder.

Mousepad night?

Next time you're at the ballpark, look around and count the billboards. All around the mezzanine level, the outfield fence, and any and everywhere else. Don't forget the ads in Japanese and Korean—they count, too. It's only a matter of time before we see ads on athletes' uniforms, like in other sports, such as car racing, golf, soccer, and tennis.

I guess it *is* progress. The Yankee payroll is often over $200 million a year. Whenever I sold beer in the stands and someone complained to me about the exorbitant prices, I often said, "Well, we gotta pay for that third baseman."

And after a brief laugh, they took a moment, nodded, and said, "Yeah. I guess you're right."

On August 16, 2006, the anniversary of Babe Ruth's death, the Yankees broke ground on their present ballpark, and I was there. Some of us vendors were invited and asked to evoke a game atmosphere by passing out peanuts to the invited crowd seated in some makeshift bleachers. Along with George Steinbrenner, principal owner of the Yankees, there was New York Governor George Pataki, Mayor Michael Bloomberg, various other politicians, former ballplayers, and celebrities (Billy Crystal was there) all sharing in the overlapping of two eras. Each of us grabbed a shovel that day and tossed a little commemorative dirt for the groundbreaking in an area that is now deep center field in the new stadium.

I grab a shovel at the groundbreaking

I remember Mr. Steinbrenner sitting for two hours in the broiling hot sun. When it was his turn to speak, he could only muster enough strength to thank everyone for being there and wish the new ballpark well. In retrospect, with his passing in the summer of 2010, this day of the groundbreaking was where I saw the early decline of "The Boss" and his bluster.

During the ceremony, the borough president, Adolfo Carrión Jr., stated, "This was a great day for the Bronx." He'd hoped this new building would spark more jobs and more revenue for his borough and the surrounding neighborhood. Years earlier, I'd had a meeting with his predecessor, Fernando Ferrer. Before Steinbrenner signed on for the new ballpark, he had threatened to move the team to New Jersey, Manhattan, or even Connecticut, of all places. I had met one of Mr. Ferrer's aides at a game and told him I had many suggestions for helping to keep the Yankees in the Bronx. After a series of phone calls, a meeting was set up between the borough president and me.

That particular day, I sat in his office in the Bronx County Courthouse with him and his aide and offered some of my ideas. I suggested putting up a "Hall of Heroes" display at the 161st Street subway platform, to commemorate Yankee greats of the past with photos and memorabilia, protected against vandalism in a sturdy enclosed casing. I proposed he have a direct train run from Grand Central Station up to Yankee Stadium, non-stop. "Take the train to the game... in only ten minutes!"

I thought, if he convinced good restaurants to open up in the area—not just typical bar food, but good-quality restaurants—it would help the Yankees, the Bronx, and even the neighborhood.

As I rattled off my ideas, Mr. Ferrer scoffed at every one. "Oh, we thought of that," he would say. But I also noticed out of the corner of my eye that his aide was jotting down everything I said. And many of my ideas are, in fact, part of the new ballpark's selling points: a commuter train now runs directly to 161st Street, and a high-end steak house is in the new park, though I doubt my meeting years earlier had anything to do with it, but you never know.

The original Yankee Stadium opened in 1923 and was renovated in 1974-75. During the renovation, the Yankees played their home games at the Mets' Shea Stadium, and it never did feel or look right. The team was mediocre, and there was a strange karma, seeing the Yankees playing home games in Queens. For me, the fit was so wrong and awkward I didn't bother to go out there to work. I simply took off those two years, opting to work in the Catskills, so my run at the big ballpark actually had a two-year hiccup in it, though I did manage to maintain my seniority.

Incidentally, when the Mets and Yankees played in the 2000 subway series, I did go out to Shea to work a few playoff games, since they were shorthanded for staff, so I guess I *was* a "lifer," however briefly.

My last day vending at Shea was rather unceremonious, as I was assigned hot dogs even though I had been assured I'd be selling beer, the more lucrative product, like I had in the previous few games. I went up to the foreman prior to the start of the game. He'd been a long-time Shea vendor many years earlier who had moved up the corporate ladder. Unfortunately, he loved to take his angst out on his employees. I told him I thought I would be getting beer, as promised, mentioning that I hadn't sold hot dogs in at least ten years.

His sarcastic response: "It's easy. You just open a bun and shove a dog in there." I handed in my badge and walked out of Shea for good.

When Citi Field opened, some of my fellow vendors who work both ballparks passed some news on to me about that particular foreman. It seems, when they designed the Mets' new ballpark, they neglected to build an office for him. "Mr. Met," the Mets mascot with the enormous, size-40 head, somehow managed to rate an office, but this foreman did not. "Shove a dog in there." Indeed.

In its final days, I was very aware that Yankee Stadium was eighty-five years old. When I was in the locker room changing into my vending uniform, I would look up and see paint peeling all around me, while timeworn pipes were held together with string. Blue-colored duct tape did its best to conceal the fact that the leather seats, after years of sitting in the bright sun down the left field side, were cracking, and there was little fiscal sense in repairing the damage. It was sad to see the stadium go out a little tarnished like that.

Back in the seventies, eighties, and nineties, the stadium's expanse and the comfort it afforded its crowds seemed to work just fine. But today, we are a little bit larger, and the aisles of the ballpark seemed to have shrunk just a tad. When I was attending games as a kid, I bought a soda that came in a twelve-ounce cup. Now, we drink Big Gulps that are a quart-sized thirty-two ounces and sometimes larger. And when I was younger, popcorn came in a tiny bag or sometimes in a funnel that, when emptied, could also double as a megaphone to cheer on the team. And the buckets of popcorn sold at the ballpark nowadays? A baby can probably take a bath in that thing.

The final season takes its toll

There is a phrase in the 21st century that goes, "Fifty is the new forty," meaning that fifty-year-olds are fit enough now to live life like a forty-year-old from years past. I also think that "230 is the new 180," meaning that people who used to be 180 pounds are now 230 pounds. And why shouldn't we be 230 pounds? We consume large amounts of food, especially at the ballpark: foot-long hot dogs, quarts of soft drinks, and jumbo everything.

In the stands and aisles, I have had to squeeze around hefty fans by pivoting on my heel, my toe, and the side of my sneakers. I have nuzzled around moms carrying babies, plump grandmas, and overweight thugs all because the space was too tight to maneuver.

The new stadium's larger aisles and corridors help ease the congestion for all of the chain restaurants and food merchants. Vendors, with our more limited variety of items to sell, could soon become a thing of the past. Years ago, I went to a newly built ballpark and barely had a sense there was a game going on, with stores and shops trying to lure the fans into buying something they didn't realize they needed until just that minute. I told friends it was such a gigantic food mall, if "you went down the wrong aisle, you might actually see the game."

The Yankees allowed corporations to promote their wares in the old stadium, so one could get a free blanket or towel for signing up for a new credit card. I can recall entering or leaving the ballpark and being handed all kinds of new items that were hitting the market, from soft drinks to cigarettes to keychains to posters to T-shirts to any number of items.

Now, some teams have taken it to a new level. The Indianapolis Colts have a hallway at their home stadium filled with dishwashers, washing machines, and refrigerators, in case one would like to go shopping during halftime. Apparently, there are even sponsors loaning their names for gates and entrances with fees paid for the privilege. The trend recently has been to have a corporation get naming rights to a ballpark, and, since the Colts' Stadium cost $719 million, the team has to make its money back somehow, so it is now known as Lucas Oil Stadium.

Though the Steinbrenner family refused to sell naming rights the way the Mets went with Citi Field for their ballpark, the new era began on April 16, 2009, when the gates opened at 1 East 161st Street, the present home of Yankee Stadium. Many felt the team didn't need the extra revenue for naming rights, since they were getting many tax credits from the city. Tax "credits" actually means it was built with taxpayer money, a final figure that we will never really know. *The New York Times* reported in

2009 that the city's comptroller did an audit and claimed the Yankees owed $11.3 million in back rent, which the team agreed to pay. Fans were anxious to see where their money had been spent, and it appears the crowds are enjoying what may be forever known as The House That Jeter Built.

Opening a can in the old stadium

The old stadium had ramps throughout, no steps, and, after the renovation in the seventies, escalators. There was also access to a few elevators for handicapped and elderly patrons, and it had a cozy feel to it. The new stadium is grand, a wide-open space with large concourses for the fans to roam freely. There is a Yankee museum, where artifacts include old photographs and news clippings; historical highlights of the team, and even Thurman Munson's old locker, all prominently displayed. It is a must-see for any baseball fan. The Great Hall is also impressive, with its large banners of Yankee greats hanging as one enters the ballpark. There is no denying that the new stadium, with a mix of old and new, is an overwhelming sight.

Beyond any other change in the ballpark, there is the food. The new Yankee Stadium caters to its fans' appetites more than anything else. No longer will a hot dog and a beer do for "the greatest fans in the world." When I came to a game in the sixties, if I wanted something special to eat, there was a stand downstairs on the first base side. There, a tall man wearing a large white chef's hat stood on a platform and carved out corned beef and roast beef for sandwiches on rye. They came with a pickle, there was usually a long line, and this was the only place in the whole ballpark where a fan could get something exotic, and by that I mean a sandwich.

In the final few years of the old ballpark, a Food Court was installed on the field level, which offered fried chicken, burgers, some meat sandwiches, and even Chinese food. The new stadium's menu keeps changing year to year, but it has offered sushi rolls, bison burgers, gourmet steak sandwiches, bar-b-que pulled pork or brisket, short ribs, various chicken dishes, caramelized onion French dip sandwiches, crispy Buffalo cauliflower buns, nachos, sliders, candied apples, and a peanut butter and jelly sandwich for the kids. A full balanced assortment of comfort food, as opposed to what many of us veterans in the old stadium referred to as "dis-comfort" food.

At the new ballpark, the marketing department works overtime on imaginative terminology. Since the upper deck or grandstand is now known as "Terrace Seating," it's no surprise that one can now have an old-time Ballantine, Schaefer, or Pabst Blue Ribbon beer at the "retro" stand. What was once a long forgotten brew is now a hip, trendy beer. Fans can also go to Beers of the World to get an import or craft beer or to one of many bars to grab a mimosa, a mojito, or anything else the bartenders can think of. Still not satisfied? Sit down for a meal while the lineups are being announced at the Hard Rock Café, conveniently located off the Great Hall near home plate. If entertaining a client, then head to NYY, the white-linen steakhouse on the second level that offers surf and turf, high-end rib eyes, and Alaskan king crabs.

One fan I met wasn't very enthused or amused by the onslaught of commercialism. He was a long-time season ticket holder who was amazed how all of the TV sets throughout the stadium spend more time showing the various kitchens and food stations busily preparing their wares than showing highlights from the games. As I was selling him a scorecard, he told me he had gone into the bathroom and heard a broadcast through speakers in there. On his visit, however, a guest chef from the food channel was explaining over the air the proper way to make lobster bisque. In the bathroom. I loved his reaction to that whole episode. He looked up at me behind my scorecard stand and simply said, "Huh?"

The Yankees like to put an "official" stamp on their corporate partnerships, so there is now an "official" snack food of the Yankees, an "official" water, an "official" ice cream, an "official" deli meat—even an "official" pudding. It won't be long before fans hear the voice of a vendor bellowing, "Hey, get your pudding here! Official Yankee pudding here!"

Back in the late seventies and eighties, I took the liberty of calling my product the "official beer of the Yankees," with the tag line, "Billy Martin's favorite." Like the former Bronx borough president, maybe somebody upstairs stole my idea.

Of course, it's been highly publicized how pricey the tickets have become. When the prime locations in the front row proved to be a little steep for the economic times, at $2500 a seat, the team decided to cut their price in half to $1250.

"I don't know, honey. What do you think? Should we go see the Yanks play the White Sox or put the kids through college...?"

The vendors now refer to the old stadium as "across the street." During batting practice, fans there were permitted to come downstairs and hug the railing to cheer on their favorite players, occasionally corralling one or two for an autograph. Once "BP" ended, these fans, mostly kids, had to go back to their assigned seats, but they were thrilled to be able to even briefly see their heroes up close.

Early in the opening season of the new ballpark, the chief operating officer of the Yankees unfortunately decided he didn't want the young fans coming down to observe batting practice. According to the C.O.O., these seats on the field level are now "sacrosanct."

"If you were to buy a new house," he was quoted as saying, "you don't want anyone coming into your house." Two days later, management wisely came to their senses and changed the policy. If this had occurred under George Steinbrenner's reign, when he was mightily in charge, he not only would have changed the policy, he would have changed the C.O.O.

In the opening months, more problems ensued. At a Boston Red Sox game, a two-hour rain delay resulted in some employees telling fans the game was going to be postponed, so some of those fans left the ballpark. When they got to a neighborhood bar, they found out from a broadcast that the game was, in fact, going to resume, but when they tried to get back in, they were told, "Once you exit, you can't return." Ah, the corporate mentality raising its itsy-bitsy head.

I always believe in making decisions on a case-by-case basis. That's a concept some authority figures are unfamiliar with. "If I let you in, I have to let everybody in." Uh, Einstein... No, you don't. These people with ticket stubs were stuck during a long rain delay, and now they may never come back to a game, thanks to "corporate policy." Think about it. Hundreds of dollars for a ticket, driving all the way in from Connecticut, parking for thirty-five dollars, and a Yankee employee with a sign that reads, "How Can I Help You?" says the game is going to be cancelled. They leave, and then later head back only to be told they can't come in. For lack of a better word—"Huh?"

The attitude of management, as well as the high cost of tickets, has probably factored into the lack of emotion and excitement on the part of the fans downstairs behind home plate and the dugouts. With so many empty seats, it gives the impression the fans are sitting in the first class section of a trans-Atlantic flight. There they are, spread apart, casually filing their nails, supping on exotic foods, and looking and appearing bored. The fans behind the Yankee dugout don't cheer; they strike a pose. And the Yankee brass probably couldn't care less, since their brand name is worth billions, as is their cable TV contract.

Across the street, I had a lot of freedom and really didn't answer to my employer, only to the fan asking me for a beer. Once vending was overseen by corporate owners, there were now a lot of bosses with walkie-talkies telling me where to stand, how to talk to fans, and what color shirt to wear underneath my uniform. Losing autonomy has taken the spirit from many of the vendors.

I overheard one old timer in the locker room say, "Somebody is telling me how to do my job who's never done it before. Let them carry a tray around to a crowd of idiots, and then they might remotely know what the hell we're talking about."

Security has, of course, been heightened, as well. In the years since 9/11, metal detectors were installed at the old stadium, and we employees had to file through these detectors and have our bags checked whenever we entered the building. Now, it is a bit more sophisticated process, but I laughed when security half-heartedly checked my clear, see-through bags without really even looking properly. I could, in fact, have had something dangerous in there, but they didn't really know what to look for. Word has it that a newly hired chef for one of the luxury restaurants was fired early in the season and came back the next day, brandishing an attitude and a sword! I hope the metal detector picked up that one.

Needless to say, the transition for me from across the street was a bit rough. As a beer vendor in the new venue, I was required to ID every person I sold a beer to… every single time I sold him or her a beer. I had to ask for proof from a seventy-six-year old wearing a "Korean Veteran" hat. It was quite absurd, but to ease the tension, I told him he didn't look a day over nineteen. I even had to refuse a fan who claimed he was fifty-nine because he didn't have ID. People lie about being twenty-one, but no one lies about being fifty-nine!

The problem with this policy is that it obviously becomes annoying to the fans. Oftentimes, I needed a row of people to pass me a wallet with an ID in it, which can be coming from a person I may have actually sold a beer to three innings earlier. I have even said to some fans, "Look, Steve, I know you're from Teaneck, and I know you're thirty-two, but I still need to see proof... Again."

And the reason I needed to proof the same people is that the company I worked for was taking pictures of me doing my due diligence, as unnecessary as that diligence may have been. I do enough silly things on my own; I don't need someone else forcing me to do more of them. But there's that itsy-bitsy head again, doing its thing.

When people enter the ballpark, I think there should be a stand where they can show proper identification and receive a snug wristband that is not transferable. I have seen this at concert venues, and it can work effectively at the stadium. If someone had come in and bypassed the stand but later decided, "Now, yes, I would like a beer," he or she could go to another stand in the hallway and sign up. Less inconvenience for the fans, less stress on the vendors, more money for the company, and legal issues would all be properly taken care of.

One game, I asked a middle-aged fan for his ID for the second time in three innings, and he was not happy. He was well built, about five foot eight, but tough and grizzled looking, quite possibly an ex-con with a flattop haircut and a string of tattoos on his arm. He was a no-nonsense guy; let's leave it at that. He stared at me as he was taking out his wallet for the second time and growled, "I will do this now, but <u>*do not*</u> ask me for proof again. **<u>UNDERSTAND?</u>**" Oh, I understood. And to avoid any problems, I didn't go down his section again for the rest of the game. Not once.

The lower deck has become a very difficult place to sneak into, which is sorry news for the average New York City fan. Each time someone gets up to buy something or go to the bathroom, they must retain their ticket stub to get back to their seat. I am reminded of two friends of mine who were seated behind the Yankee dugout in the old stadium. When I saw them, I said, "Boogie, Matt, how'd you get these seats?"

Both of them looked around and quickly whispered, "*Ssshh!* Not so loud! We paid an usher a few bucks."

The ushers used to be a traditional fixture at a game. They greeted the fans and took them to their section, wiping down the seats with large gloves that were like furry oven mitts. They would shine those seats up, front and back and underneath, then wait as long as it took for the fan to give them a subway, usually a buck or two. To vendors, however, the ushers were in *our* way and we were in *their* way, though we had a mutual respect for one another in terms of trying to eke out a living. Until George Steinbrenner got rid of these older men—and I mean old, since very few were under seventy—they were a major part of the fabric of the stadium. However, they often were on the take, eager to make a few extra bucks to let anyone into some empty seats down low.

Back to Boogie and Matt. I returned a few innings later to their section, and they were gone, but two other guys were sitting in the seats. I assumed my buddies were chased. *Not unusual*, I thought. Used to happen all the time when we were kids.

Another two innings later, I came back, and there's Boogie and Matt. "What happened?" I asked.

And Boogie told me, "We went up to go to the bathroom and when we got back, these two teenagers were in our seats. We called the usher over, the guy whose palms we'd greased earlier. He asked the kids where their tickets were, and the kids said, 'Wait a second. Where are these guys' tickets?' Now that pissed the usher off and he went nuts. 'Never mind about them. Where the hell are your tickets?' And he tossed them out... So we got back in."

Now *that* kind of thing cannot happen in the new ballpark. No way. No how. It's a shame, don't ya think?

I must admit, however, some of the old stadium's charm *has* been maintained. When fans step off the subway, they can still look up at the façade and see American League team flags flying in the wind. Every day, the flags are positioned in the order of the standings, so if the Yanks are playing Cleveland, for instance, one could see exactly what place the Indians are in in their division. It's a nice touch that has been kept up. On Saturday games, the loudspeakers still blare "Saturday, In the Park" by the band Chicago, and Sunday's tune remains Bobby Darin's "Sunday In New York," as fans leisurely watch batting practice, basking in the sun with their huge, multi-sectioned *New York Times* in their laps. Nice traditions that have been preserved.

The old ticket booths, where you had to pay in cash

I can't deny there is still a palpable energy that flows through the new ballpark. Just before the gates open, cotton candy is being freshly spun and placed on large boards for the vendors to sell, as it has been for decades. The aromas of grilled food and popcorn emanate from section to section. Handcarts are pushed from the elevators, rolled over to various stations, while instructions are barked out on walkie-talkies. Employees prepare for the sound of the metal gates opening and the fans scurrying in to their sections with wide-eyed enthusiasm. Yes, there is still excitement echoing through the hallways prior to every game.

I understand the concept of change, I really do. When I find myself in my old neighborhood in the city, I get melancholy as I think, this is where that bakery was that made that amazing apple strudel, or that's where the vet's office was where I used to take Jerome, my first cat, when he was sick. I realize that all these places go; we must let time pass on, just as Jerome did. That is simply the nature of time. People and places age, but still....

I don't know, maybe the joint across the street had just as much commercialism going on and I didn't notice it. Maybe I liked the old Yankee Stadium just fine. The ramps "going up" worked as well as any elevator or escalator, the food wasn't gourmet but it wasn't bad, either, and a bathroom was a place to go to when you had to go, not a place to get recipes for lobster bisque.

I will definitely miss it. I know progress rolls on but I don't need more corporate boxes or sushi or Maryland crab cakes at my ballpark. I don't know. That's just me.

But then again, I'm old school.

AFTERWORD

BEFORE I STARTED selling hot chocolate and peanuts in Yankee Stadium, I was a Little League catcher. I had dreams of becoming a Major League ballplayer, as many kids did and, I presume, still do. I looked forward to my games on the weekend with thoughts of the team I would be playing against and what my batting average was, always aware of the standings to know how we were doing. Back then, sports and statistics ruled my day. To later become a bit player in baseball's magical world was *my* version of a dream come true.

In the old stadium, vendors saw territory dwindle during the late nineties, as waiters and waitresses were employed to serve the lower deck. We were nudged past first and third base, and the dynamic of our relationship with the fans was forever altered. When the new location pushed us completely past the foul lines, vending became more challenging than it ever had been before.

I now foresee the day when fans will be able to order right from their seats, either with their cell phones or from a keypad on their armrest. The food and beverages will come to them in some variation of a chute, not unlike the way some people do their banking from their cars. At drive-through windows, the customer converses by speakerphone and then places a deposit or withdrawal request into a cylindrical tube that is whisked off to the teller inside the bank. The tube soon comes back with either money or a deposit receipt, and the customer is free to drive away.

The post-Smartphone world has become highly automated: we now read newspapers, watch videos, and communicate with people across the globe in less than seconds. Personal contact, such a great part of vending, will soon be replaced by some version of that bank teller's chute. With immediate service becoming more and more essential, our whims will mean place an order, slide a piece of plastic, and "voila!" Here comes a steaming hot roast beef sandwich on a poppy seed roll, extra horseradish dressing, and a fresh, cold, imported beer, as fast as possible.

America has essentially become a self-serve world in the twenty-first century. Websites prompt us to purchase our own products, pick out our own airline seats, and make our own doctor appointments. The economics of big business will simply add to the demise of vendors. Self-service will make vendors obsolete as companies cut costs by removing the middleman. Who knows? By the time you are reading this, it may have already happened.

The live game experience has changed dramatically since I first started coming to the ballpark in the sixties and into my working days in the seventies, eighties, nineties, and beyond. With elaborate choices of food, luxurious cushioned seats, and large TV screens placed throughout the stadium, the owners are doing whatever they can to make the fans feel as if they are in the comfort of their own home. Only those fortunate few who can afford the high-priced seats close to the action can get the true intimacy of the game.

I used to sneak down and razz the umpire from behind the first base line, and the ump would often have a nonverbal, and sometimes verbal, conversation with me. I yelled at third base coaches who either failed to wave a runner in when they should have or who waved a runner in when they shouldn't.

Where have you gone, Uncle Abie?
Our nation turns its lonely eyes to you.

In Yankee Stadium, ninety-five percent of the fans are one big roar, and those on the field can't hear anyone, especially with the loud speakers pitched as high as they are. The umpires, players, and coaches are in a cocoon, oblivious to the specific cheers and jeers from section 428 in the upper deck. The new stadium seems to cater to tourists, who tend to be soft-spoken and polite, as opposed to the local, vocal, die-hard Yankee fans of days gone by.

In 2012, I had a torn tendon that forced me to have surgery on my left shoulder. People asked me what caused it, and I used an excuse that I got it lifting weights in the gym, though I knew it was from my forty-plus years of lifting my product and lugging it through the stands. My right knee had acted up, as well, and it made sense, as I reached my mid-fifties, that these injuries, which I used to brush off with relative ease, were now going to affect my future as a vendor.

Late season, I stopped in to see the guys hanging out in the basement before getting their assignments for that night's game. That was the first summer since 1975 that I hadn't worked in the Bronx, and the feeling was truly odd for me. The veteran vendors looked beat, tired from a long, particularly humid homestand, but they were genuinely concerned when they asked, "How ya doin'?"

I don't think they cared so much about moving up on the seniority list, as they had when I missed some games in the past. No, I think they themselves could hear their own clocks ticking. "We might be losing one of our own" was the thought I read on their weary faces. When aging ballplayers give press conferences to announce their retirement, I always notice how moved they appear to be as they "let it go." Now I know exactly how they feel.

Before the gates opened, I strolled through the empty ballpark for a few more hellos to co-workers. I couldn't remember the last time I'd wandered through the stadium with such a sense of tranquility.

Since 1970, those hallways and aisles were *mine*. I owned them. But now, everything was different. I was a bit of a stranger on my old turf, yet it was liberating to me. There would be no more thrills of seeing "walk-off" home runs, of witnessing the nail-biting tension of a no-hitter, of seeing the Yanks crowned champions, as they were in 1996, just before I ran on the field and circled the bases.

The excitement of Yankee Stadium, as anyone who has been there might agree, is like no other. And for me, following in the footsteps of my dad, it was unique. After vending games when I was a teenager and then into my twenties, I used to linger after checking out in the seventh inning and try to find an empty seat to watch my heroes. I loved the crowds and the excitement, and I saw how ballplayers appeared to stay young forever, until they suddenly got old and vanished.

I know I will miss vending, miss kidding around with the guys in the locker room, and sharing our war stories. To be honest, I already miss selling beer from cans, kneeling and making the perfect pour, sending the beer down the row, lingering a little, looking around at nowhere, straightening out my money, hoping to pick up a little "subway" for my troubles.

I will miss figuring out what was happening during a game simply by hearing the crack of the bat and studying the looks on the fans' faces while I walked up an aisle with my back to the field. I will miss joking with those fans, sharing a laugh with the tens of thousands of Yankee customers I have encountered. Though passing a hot dog or a drink down an aisle or selling a T-shirt and a Yankee cap could have been only a small portion of the experience for *them*, it made me feel like I was part of the fabric of the game.

Baseball, like sports in general, is democratic—where no matter what any player looks like or where they are from, if they can hit or pitch well, they can earn a spot on a team and make a great living doing it. I will, of course, come back as a fan because I love the timelessness of baseball, the fact that there is no clock, and a game can literally go on forever—if no one breaks a tie, that is. The records and numbers live on, and the memories are ours... always.

Most people don't stay at one job for forty years. I often wonder why I stayed so long, "aging *gratefully*," as I used to say. There were many years when I would go to California, pursuing my acting career and I was tempted to stay there, perhaps skipping a few months in the season and risk losing my seniority or worse, my job.

I often found myself saying to people, "I can't believe I've been here fifteen years." Or, "I can't believe I've been here twenty-five years." Or, "Thirty... Thirty-five... Forty."

And invariably they would comment, "Well..., you must like it. You've been here so long."

And that's it. I liked it. I *really* liked it. I liked the passion of the crowds. I liked the bullshitting with the guys, the Spanish chicken and rice dinners after the game on 161st Street, the countless number of big, sold-out series against the Red Sox, the old-timer's games, the records broken, the bases stolen, the new hot-shot pitcher from some also-ran team coming in to New York to face the big, bad Yankees. And, of course, the excitement of a pennant race's final days, the playoffs, and World Series games... All of it.

Perhaps it's taken me this long to realize my good fortune. I got great exercise, climbing those ramps and steps. My hours weren't too bad, the pay was pretty good for those hours ("where de hell're ya gonna make dat kinda money?"), and I never really had to answer to any mean ol' boss, since blustery Steinbrenner controlled the *players*, not the *vendors*.

I had stability in the midst of my unpredictable acting life, with a Yankee schedule dictating where I needed to be on a certain day. I also worked on my voice as I touted my product, so they could hear me way over there in the back row. "Hey... Beer Here!" is as good a vocal exercise as any I learned in acting school. And more times than not, I had a lot of fun when I went to work.

People often ask me what the big takeaway was for me in my forty years in the Bronx. It can be difficult to come up with a finite answer for that question, but I know the stadium taught me that the fans, whether in the bleachers or behind home plate, were no better than I was. A high-salaried doctor, politician, or celebrity actor may be a bigshot in their personal life, but when there's no vendor in sight, he or she still must wait on line like everyone else for a hot dog and a beer.

Mel Allen, who was the Yankee broadcaster when I was growing up and who was there through good times and bad, had this to say about Yankee Stadium: "This was the place. The number one place. The Empire State building or the Grand Canyon of baseball. And every time I stepped inside of it I had to pinch myself."

From the age of fifteen until I was fifty-five, except for home and school, I spent more time at Yankee Stadium than anywhere else.

And I am forever grateful.

The old stadium

ACKNOWLEDGMENTS

THIS BOOK COULD not have been written without the unyielding support of my dear wife, Sharon March. She is a rock-solid presence in my life, and I couldn't imagine getting through my day, any day, without her.

I must thank Milt Kogan, who has been a major supporter of my efforts. Also, Mark Felson, Steve Felson, Roy Tschudy, Tony DeSantis, Ken Salzman, Chris Gesue, *Back in the Bronx* magazine, Allan Wasserman, Catherine Emanuel, California Lawyers For the Arts, Matt Cooper, Roger S. Haber, Jennifer Judkins, Mark Costiglio, P. Karl Engemann, Larry King, Ben Lipitz, George Kalinsky, Nick Toren, Carlyle King, my writing groups in Los Angeles and New York, David Weiss, and Kathryn F. Galán, for cleaning up my dangling participles and poor use of the comma.

Vendors at the stadium have given me the colorful palette for some of the stories I've tried to sketch here. So, too, have the thousands and thousands of fans whom I've served these forty years. I thank them for their quirkiness as well as their enthusiasm. I am grateful to my friends and family members who also helped shape this book and, in fact, my life.

ABOUT THE AUTHOR

STEWART J. ZULLY WAS born in the Bronx and started vending at Yankee Stadium in 1970. He has been an actor, director, writer, producer, and teacher since 1980.

His film credits include *Vice, Wolf, Malcolm X, For the Boys, New in Town,* and *The Bonfire of the Vanities.* He has guest-starred on *Blue Bloods, The Sopranos, Columbo, Married…with Children,* and most of the *Law and Order* shows. In 2003, his *Citibank* identity-theft commercial won an Emmy. Stewart has directed and taught theater in New York, California, Florida, and Canada and co-wrote and co-produced the feature film *Perfect Opposites.*

He and his wife, Sharon, live in Los Angeles.

Made in the USA
Middletown, DE
07 October 2022